Tree of Glory

Tree of Glory

Gonville ffrench-Beytagh

with Vera Hodges

Darton, Longman and Todd
London

First published in 1988 by
Darton, Longman and Todd Ltd
89 Lillie Road, London SW6 1UD

© 1988 Gonville ffrench-Beytagh and Vera Hodges

ISBN 0 232 51776 2

British Library Cataloguing in Publication Data

Ffrench-Beytagh, Gonville,
  Tree of glory.
  1. Christian life
  I. Title II. Hodges, Vera
  248.4

ISBN 0–232–51776–2

Phototypeset by Input Typesetting Ltd, London SW19 8DR
Printed and bound by Anchor Brendon Ltd, Tiptree, Essex

Contents

Foreword

Last year DLT published our book *A Glimpse of Glory* which was based on Canon Gonville ffrench-Beytagh's teaching about prayer. Our new book is based on his teaching about the crucifixion. Gonville is a ready speaker but he finds writing increasingly difficult, and it has again fallen to me to make a book out of things which he has said.

We began working in the City of London, in Gonville's high study leading out onto the roof of St Vedast-alias-Foster and looking across to the dome of St Paul's Cathedral. Then there were several months when work stopped. Illness, retirement, and house-moving brought changes to us both. I moved upriver to a place in my son-in-law's vicarage on the edge of the Cotswolds. Gonville moved from the City to Tower Hamlets in London's East End, to share a house off Mile End Road; he left the historic dignity of St Vedast's for worship in a simple basement chapel ('The broom cupboard makes an admirable sacristy!') or in the bareness of an adapted church hall. Here we took up our work in a study which looks out on plane trees round a green square. On the wall is a map of Africa, several icons, and a crucifix. There are chairs for the pilgrims who still seek him. There is a file of notes.

We began from those rather brief, often illegible, skeleton notes. Gonville talked his way through them against my constant suggestions and questions. I taped our conversations and took them home to organize in my room looking towards the fine spire of St Lawrence, Lechlade, where, as I write, the cuckoo is calling over the stripling Thames.

I was once asked what were my qualifications for editing

Gonville's work. I explained that I had two essential qualifications: I had inherited a copy of Young's *Concordance* from my grandfather and I had bought a word processor for myself. With these very practical tools I have been able to sort our material. I have tracked the quotations, cut out the stammer, finished the sentences and added the stops. Besides doing these obvious editing jobs I have brought in some fresh illustrations and expanded and rearranged passages in order to make Gonville's ideas as clear as I can. I have added words here and there for the benefit of those who are more at home with other ways of saying and doing things. High Mass at a City church is and is not the same service as a Parish Communion at Lechlade. The Authorised Version is and is not the same Bible as the NEB or the NIV. My slice of church life is different from Gonville's and I have sometimes drawn on my own reading and experience where it seemed appropriate to us both. In all this we have co-operated most happily. The introductions to each chapter are in my own voice and are set in italic.

We have broken our material into a group of short devotional readings which touch many different aspects of the Passion. Gonville's insights are often imaginative and original but they are faithful to the Christian devotional tradition. I feel emboldened in this work by the authentic atmosphere which he carries with him – by the sense that these thoughts are those of a man who has lived close to Christ and helped others to know him, who has known suffering and helped others to bear it. It has been a privilege to do my part in giving his friends, old and new, another volume of his teaching.

Lechlade   V.J.H.

Preface

When I survey the wondrous Cross
On which the Prince of Glory died . . .

I am thinking about the most important and crucial three hours in history, and I invite you to look with me at some of things that I have seen in my survey.

The Cross stands in the centre of my faith. Perhaps that was not always so, but my experiences in Africa, my days in prison and my months on remand and on trial, did much to deepen my understanding. That period gave me a new conviction of the depth of God's love and a fuller sense of the meaning of the Passion. That is one reason why two pieces about Africa have a place here.

Recently I read a book by a physicist. He marvelled at the glories of creation, the macrocosm and the microcosm and so on; then he said, 'When one thinks of it, the mind boggles. I think it is a good thing for the mind of man to boggle once a day!' I agree. I have imagined myself, after death, in some hospital in paradise where I have been sent to be made better, to convalesce from the wounds of my sins; and as evening comes on the sister walks round with her trolley of medicines, and says, 'Well, Father, has your mind boggled today?' That is not frivolous. Our Lord told us to be as little children and one of the graces of childhood is the capacity for wonder. Milton set out 'to justify the ways of God to man' – that is not my line; I would rather look at God's ways and wonder about them, then marvel at them. Wonder is one of the thresholds of prayer, and I hope there is something in this book to help the reader to the wonder which turns to worship.

I have tried to look at the scene at Calvary and at some of
the footprints through the Old Testament which lead us there.
I have tried to look through Calvary to God in his heaven. I
try to feel my way towards the meaning and method of our
redemption; but that is largely beyond me. Perhaps I understand more about how it works with my heart than with my
head, and you will find that your love will take you further than
your logic. Someone called some of this work 'A Rhapsody on
a Theme' – the theme of love. But to reach out towards the
glory of God's love we need to stretch our minds and imaginations to their utmost limit.

When we survey the dark glory of the Cross we can sometimes glimpse through it to the transcendent, translucent glory
beyond, as we see the Cross at the heart of the Holy Blessed
and Glorious Trinity. We conceive Christ, the Son of God, as
it were, at the centre of the Trinity of Father, Son, and Holy
Spirit, and the Cross, as it were, at the centre of Christ himself.
Each time that we Christians say, 'Glory be to the Father, Son
and Holy Spirit, as it was in the beginning, is now, and ever
shall be' – each time, we are proclaiming the glory of the Cross.

The Cross is in the centre of Christ's meaning for us. As we
worship 'Jesus Christ the same yesterday, and today, and for
ever' (Heb. 13:8), we see his Cross in the context of time past,
time present, and time to come. This idea threads through my
meditations as I consider the Cross from different points of
view.

My meditations have grown into this book of devotional
readings. Here are various aspects of the Cross which I have
found fruitful. I hope that they will yield some fruit to others
who look for suitable fare for Lent and Holy Week. I would
suggest that you should take a little at a time and turn it over
slowly in your mind and heart, and may God be with you as
you do so.

Tredegar Square   G.ff.B.
London E3

Biographical Notes

Gonville ffrench-Beytagh was born in 1912 in Shanghai, the son of an Irish business man. ('Beytagh' is an Irish name pronounced like 'beater'.) His parents separated, and when he was nine he was sent to England in the care of a woman teacher who became his guardian. He went to Monkton Combe School and Bristol Grammar School. When he was sixteen he went to New Zealand to join an agricultural school, but he was quickly expelled after a midnight escapade. He ran away from the job which was found for him and, at the age when most future ecclesiastics are studying for examinations at school or university, Gonville was bumming round New Zealand as a tramp and casual labourer, getting into fights, dodging the police, milking cows, and shearing sheep.

He had lost contact with his family, but an unexpected meeting with a relative led to help for a passage to South Africa. There he was out of work for a period but eventually found a job in an office in Johannesburg. There he met Toc H and gave some help to their boys' clubs; but he was an irreverent agnostic and kept apart from the religious side of their life.

The home in Shanghai had been completely pagan, and the churches which Gonville had met in England had led to a determination never, of his own will, to attend another. The turning point came when he was attacked by muggers in a subway and received a blow, probably from an iron bar, which broke his jaw. One of his Toc H friends – Alan Paton, the author of *Cry, the Beloved Country* – at once came to see him in hospital. Gonville had to stay there for some time, and this gave him opportunity (as Alan Paton put it) 'to reflect on the nature and destiny of man and the nature and lack of destiny of himself'. What sort of person did he want to be? Had the lively Christians whom he had met through Toc H more to show him than the carefree, adventurous, Bulldog Drummond types whom he had previously admired? When he came out of hospital he began to attend services. He was barely a Christian when he knew that he must be a priest. He talked to Bishop (later Archbishop) Geoffrey Clayton, who was to become a great friend and influence, and some substitute for the close family which he had never known. A year after leaving hospital he joined St Paul's Theological College in Grahamstown.

Gonville resented the restrictions of life in the theological college but stuck it out with impatience. He was ordained in 1939 and served in several places in the Diocese of Johannesburg. There is ample evidence of the deep influence of his ministry as a parish priest. For a time he was chaplain of a sisterhood while acting as Diocesan Missioner and doing more administrative work than he enjoyed. In 1955 he was invited to Rhodesia as Dean of Salisbury Cathedral.

In 1965 he went back to Johannesburg as Dean of St Mary's Cathedral. He had gradually come to see South Africa's apartheid system as utterly unchristian and he was determined to show his people that it was contrary to God's love, and to bring black and white together, at least in his cathedral. He pleased some and enraged others. He faced petty persecution and, in January 1971, he was arrested and charged with subversion under the South African Terrorism Act. After a long trial he was convicted and sentenced to five years imprisonment; but the sentence was quashed on appeal.

It seemed clear that he would not be allowed to continue working in South Africa, but he saw that he could serve the country by lecturing and writing about the true nature of apartheid. His book *Encountering Darkness* gives his view of the system with which he clashed. He was already an Honorary Canon of Johannesburg and in 1973, after settling in England, he was made an Honorary Canon of Canterbury. For a short period he was an assistant priest at St Matthew's, Westminster, and in 1974 he became Rector of St Vedast-alias-Foster, a church in the City of London.

He retired from St Vedast's at Christmas 1986 and now lives with four friends in Tower Hamlets. They belong to the congregation of Holy Trinity, Mile End, whose church is too dilapidated for use. They support its Sunday service in a Methodist hall and keep a daily celebration of the Eucharist in their own chapel.

Vera Hodges was born in the same year as Canon ffrench-Beytagh in a Worcestershire vicarage. She was educated at Christ's Hospital, Hertford, and Reading University. She married Professor H. A. Hodges, who lectured and wrote on both philosophy and theology and who often represented the Church of England at ecumenical conferences. Vera Hodges taught at Kendrick Girls' Grammar School in Reading and, after her husband's death, studied church history at King's College, London. She then became a reader and tutor to candidate readers in the Diocese of Oxford.

Note on Sources

Common quotations from the Bible, especially of poetical passages, are generally based on the Authorised Version (1611). Modern translations have also been used for their freshness or greater clarity. I find the NIV (New International Version) particularly attractive; I have also drawn on RV (Revised Version), RSV (Revised Standard Version), NEB (New English Bible), GNB (Good News Bible) and LB (Living Bible).

Prayers are quoted from BCP (Book of Common Prayer 1662), ASB (Alternative Service Book 1980) and LHWE (Services for Lent, Holy Week and Easter 1984).

Hymns are quoted from AMR (Hymns Ancient and Modern Revised), EH (English Hymnal), and MHB (Methodist Hymn Book).

V.J.H.

When I survey the wondrous Cross
  On which the Prince of glory died,
My richest gain I count but loss
  And pour contempt on all my pride.

Forbid it, Lord, that I should boast
  Save in the death of Christ my God;
All the vain things that charm me most,
  I sacrifice them to his Blood.

See from his head, his hands, his feet,
  Sorrow and love flow mingled down;
Did e'er such love and sorrow meet,
  Or thorns compose so rich a crown?

His dying crimson like a robe,
  Spreads o'er his body on the Tree;
Then am I dead to all the globe,
  And all the globe is dead to me.

Were the whole realm of nature mine,
  That were a present far too small;
Love so amazing, so divine,
  Demands my soul, my life, my all.
                (Isaac Watts, 1707)

But God forbid that I should glory, save in the cross of our Lord Jesus Christ, by whom the world is crucified unto me, and I unto the world. (Gal. 6:14)

Him hath God exalted with his right hand to be a Prince and a Saviour, for to give repentance to Israel, and forgiveness of sins.   (Acts 5:31)

1

As It Was in the Beginning

The whole Bible tells of the love of God and helps us to under-
stand the supreme act of love in Jesus' Crucifixion. This book
moves from Genesis to Revelation but it always keeps close to
Calvary. The early concepts of the Hebrews, shown in their
stories, their poetry and their practices, increase in significance
as we see how they point towards the Cross. And looking back
from the Cross we trace the loving purpose of God at work from
the beginning.

The Tree of Life

It is recorded in the book of Genesis (2:9) that at man's beginning the Lord God planted a garden and there he put the man
he had formed. And God made all kinds of trees grow out of
the ground – trees that were pleasing to the eye and good for
food. In the middle of the garden were two particular trees,
the tree of the knowledge of good and evil and the tree of life.
The tree of the knowledge of good and evil was attractive, but
God said, 'You are free to eat from any tree of the garden;
but you must not eat from the tree of the knowledge of good
and evil.' But, as you know, the serpent tempted Eve who
tempted Adam. They both ate fruit from the tree and were
cast out of the garden. God said, 'He must not be allowed to
reach out his hand and take also from the tree of life and eat,
and live for ever.' And God set cherubim on the east side of
Eden and 'a flaming sword flashing back and forth to guard the
way to the tree of life'.

Adam and Eve were not originally warned off the tree of life. It gets barely a mention, but God did not intend them to have access to it after they had tasted the tree of the knowledge of good and evil. They would abuse their knowledge and turn to evil; they were not ready for the tree of life.

Of course this is a legend, a myth, a parable, but it no less tells the truth. The story of man can be conceived as being his struggle to get back to the tree of life, to find the philosopher's stone, to reach immortality, to drink from the spring of eternal youth or the elixir of life. This is an archetypal theme. It is a characteristic of the nature of man that he longs for life and meaning. He longs for the tree of life.

Now, on Good Friday, we look upon the real tree of life. There *is* something which will give man eternity, and our interpretation is that that is the Cross. There is a subconscious feeling in these stories that somewhere there is a source of eternal life, and we are saying, 'Yes, that is true. This longing for eternity is not just a primitive yearning. There is in fact such a thing as a tree of life. It is the Cross.'

> God in pity saw man fallen,
>   Shamed and sunk in misery,
> When he fell on death by tasting
>   Fruit of the forbidden tree;
> Then another tree was chosen
>   Which the world from death should free.

The hymn goes on almost to identify the cross with our Lord who hangs there, as its fruit and blossom:

> Faithful Cross! above all other,
>   One and only noble tree!
> None in foliage, none in blossom,
>   None in fruit thy peer may be.
>   (Venantius, tr. Percy Dearmer, EH 95)

And Jesus saw himself as a tree of life. Our Lord says 'I am the vine' – and that is a kind of tree: 'I am the vine' (John 15:5) and 'I am come that they might have life, and have it abundantly' (John 10:10).

God's Loving Purpose

Immediately man – 'Adam' means man – had sinned and come short of the glory to which he was destined, God responded in love; but that response is spread out in time, through Abraham, through Moses, through the prophets. God goes on reaching down to man and finally his great dart of longing love, Christ himself, like an arrow or a spear, is shot from the heart of God. 'A spear anchoring the absolute,' said someone – locking eternity into time and space. He plunged down from heaven into mankind and locked into the earth like a great harpoon by which we can be drawn back to God himself.

At the beginning of the annual carol Service of Nine Lessons broadcast from King's College, Cambridge, we hear the Bidding Prayer with these words: 'Let us read and mark in Holy Scripture the tale of the loving purposes of God from the first days of our disobedience unto the glorious redemption wrought for us by this Holy Child.'

Our redemption was wrought on the Cross. The Cross was the central point and purpose of the Incarnation. Jesus was born so that he could be crucified. It was not just an incident or accident in his life – 'For this purpose came I unto this hour' (John 12:27). In the Nicene Creed we proclaim our belief in Jesus Christ, 'Who for us men and our salvation came down from heaven and was incarnate by the Holy Ghost of the Virgin Mary, and was crucified also for us under Pontius Pilate.' It was for 'our salvation' that he came and suffered, and was glad to suffer. Jesus 'for the joy that was set before him endured the cross, scorning its shame' (Heb. 12:2). Our salvation is his joy, and it is the theme of the Bible from Genesis to Revelation. It arches all history from the creation to the consummation of all things.

The Cross is the exact centre of our faith. We can locate a precise point in time and place when and where our salvation was wrought:

Then came, at a predetermined moment, a moment in time and of time,

A moment not out of time, but in time, in what we call
　　history: transecting, bisecting the world of time, a
　　moment in time but not like a moment of time,
A moment in time but time was made through that moment:
　　for without the meaning there is no time, and that
　　moment of time gave the meaning.
　　　　　　　　　　　　　　(T. S. Eliot, 'The Rock')

The Bible centres in the Cross. We may stand by it to look
back to the creation, to Adam and to Abraham, to 'the goodly
fellowship of the Prophets'. We look forward from the Cross
to 'the noble army of Martyrs and the holy Church throughout
all the world'. We look from the Cross to our own time, to the
end of time, and to the vision of God. The Cross is the central,
focal, point in the great story of our salvation.

His Only Son

Let us look at some Old Testament foreshadowings of God's
plan. First, obviously, there is the story of Abraham and Isaac
which turned out to be a non-event. Our church has seen it as
foreshadowing the Cross; the story is read at Matins on Good
Friday. Isaac was miraculously born of an old mother (as Christ
was miraculously conceived, 'born of the virgin Mary'). The
Lord promised Abraham that in his seed, his descendants, all
the families of the earth should be blessed. Suddenly God told
Abraham to sacrifice Isaac, his only son. 'Take now thy son,
thine only son Isaac, whom thou lovest . . . and offer him for
a burnt offering' (Gen. 22:2). If Isaac was killed there would
be no seed, no descendants. So Abraham in blind obedience
takes Isaac to sacrifice him on the mountain. He binds him on
the altar and lifts his knife to kill his son. He hears the voice
of God, 'Abraham. Abraham, lay not thine hand upon thy son,
thine only son.' And Isaac's life is saved. And in his seed have
all the nations of the earth been blessed, because Jesus, son of
God, was also a descendant of Abraham.
　　Now an important element in the story has been left out –

the clue to the whole thing. As Abraham and Isaac trudged to the mountain carrying wood and fire, Isaac said, 'Behold the fire and the wood, but where is the lamb for the burnt offering?' (Gen. 22:7). Abraham said, 'My son, God will provide himself with a lamb,' and so in the fullness of time, God did exactly that; when the time was ripe he provided his only Son to be the lamb, the lamb of God. This was not a non-event: it was *the* event. And this time the sacrifice was completed and consummated on the Cross on Calvary. Jesus gave himself for 'all the families of the earth' – 'The bread that I will give is my flesh, which I will give for the life of the world' (John 6:51).

There is an earlier story about Abraham which Christians have sometimes read as a symbol of things to come. I have a Russian icon on the wall of my study, Rublev's fifteenth-century icon of the Trinity. It represents – on one level – the three men, or angels, who came to visit Abraham, and – on another level – the Father, the Son and the Holy Spirit. 'And the Lord appeared unto him in the plains of Mamre: and he sat in the tent door in the heat of the day; and he lift up his eyes and looked, and lo, three men stood by him' (Gen. 18:1,2). Abraham welcomed the strangers and killed a tender calf for them and, when they had eaten, 'the Lord' pronounced the promise of a son, for 'Abraham shall surely become a great and mighty nation, and all the nations of the earth shall be blessed in him' (Gen. 18:18). The icon shows the three 'men' round the table where the calf has been set out for them; but the calf is an image of sacrifice. The Father invites the Son to partake, and the Son, with the silent support of the Spirit, stretches out his hand to accept.

The Passover

After the Day of Atonement the other great feast in the Jewish calendar is the Passover, which celebrates the most vivid event in Jewish history. After 400 years of captivity and slavery in Egypt finally God brought about deliverance and freedom. Moses their leader approached Pharoah the king and asked,

'Let my people go.' Despite a series of devastating plagues Pharoah refused and refused to let them go – until the final plague. The Lord told Moses that on a certain night, 'Every firstborn son in Egypt will die, from the firstborn son of Pharaoh who sits on the throne, to the firstborn son of the slave girl who is at her hand mill' (Exod. 11:5). On that night every Hebrew household was told to take and kill a lamb – one for each family – and daub the blood on the doorposts and lintel of the house so that the angel of death could see the blood and pass over, so that there would be no death among the Israelites. The eldest sons of the Egyptians died, including Pharoah's son, and then the Egyptians were ready to let the Israelites go; indeed, they were ready to drive them out. Down the years until the present day the Jews have celebrated the Passover, eating a lamb and retelling the story of how God brought their forefathers out of slavery in Egypt.

It looks as if Jesus, knowing that he was doomed, deliberately determined to delay his death until the time of the Passover. He believed then that his hour had come, so that his own death on the Cross might be close to the time when the passover lamb was killed. Our Lord's thoughts and mind in the last days were clearly filled with thoughts of the Passover. He clearly identified himself with the passover lamb, especially at the Last Supper. So the Cross becomes the final slaying of the passover lamb. And the early Church saw his death in this way. Paul wrote to the Corinthians, 'Christ our passover is sacrificed for us' (1 Cor. 5:7), and we have taken the words into our Easter worship.

And at his death our great deliverance begins; our exodus, our redemption from the results of sin and eternal death. And we set out through the wilderness of life towards the promised land. On our journey we are fed with manna – with the bread of the Eucharist. This is for us the daily or weekly application of the deliverance achieved and obtained once for all upon the Cross – where Christ called out, 'It is finished,' for his great redemption was accomplished.

Two Covenants

After the children of Israel's deliverance from Egypt and the crossing of the Red Sea, we read the dramatic account of their encounter with God at Mount Sinai:

> There were thunders and lightnings, and a thick cloud upon the mount, and the voice of the trumpet exceeding loud; so that all the people that was in the camp trembled . . . And mount Sinai was altogether on a smoke, because the Lord descended upon it in fire . . .   (Exod. 19:16, 18)

Moses heard God speak on the mountain and 'told the people all the words of the Lord . . . and all the people answered with one voice, and said, All the words which the Lord hath said will we do.' And they built an altar and sacrificed oxen there and sprinkled blood on the people and on the altar. And Moses said, 'Behold the blood of the covenant, which the Lord hath made with you . . . and the glory of the Lord abode upon mount Sinai, and the cloud covered it six days . . .' (Exod. 24:3, 8, 16)

So the first covenant was made between God and his people. They should look to him and keep his commandments and obey his voice. If they served him aright God would protect them and bring them to the place prepared for them. Years later, one of the prophets summed up the covenant: 'I will be the God of all the families of Israel and they shall be my people' (Jer. 31:1).

Notice the parts of this story which link us with the New Testament story of the new covenant. Notice the dark cloud which covered Mount Sinai and suggested the presence and power of God. The cloud covered the mount just as darkness covered Mount Calvary at the crucifixion. 'Now from the sixth hour there was darkness over all the land unto the ninth hour' (Matt. 27:45). There was darkness from 12 o'clock until 3 o'clock. On both occasions the darkness, the cloud, seem to hide the glory of what was being done behind the scenes.

On Mount Sinai the covenant was ratified between God and his people; the commitment between God and Israel was sealed with a sacrifice. As the Old Testament covenant was sealed in blood on Mount Sinai so the New Testament covenant was sealed in blood – the precious blood of Jesus – on the Cross on the hill of Calvary. The blood which Christ lost and gave for us in his passion and death was symbolized at the Last Supper and is re-presented in every Eucharist. The old covenant at Sinai marked a new relationship between God and his people. The new covenant marks a new and deeper relationship with us. As the Israelites broke their side of the covenant again and again, so we break our side and are disobedient, but week by week we may renew our covenant with our Lord at Communion.

It is a pity that the word for covenant has been translated 'testament', as in, 'This cup is the new testament in my blood' (1 Cor. 11:25 AV). The newer translations are clearer; compare it with 'This cup is God's new covenant sealed with my blood' (GNB). 'For this is my blood of the new testament, which is shed for many for the remission of sins' (Matt. 26:28 AV); compare, 'For this is my blood, the blood of the covenant, shed for many for the forgiveness of sins' (NEB). Similarly the word 'covenant' is commonly used at the Holy Communion: 'Drink this, all of you; this is my blood of the new covenant . . .' (ASB).

The whole concept of covenant between God and man is rich in ideas and insights. Here is just one! Men and women are bound into families by blood relationships. There is a widespread primitive idea that men of different families or tribes or nations can become blood brothers by letting their blood flow together. So in sharing, partaking, of the precious blood of Jesus in Communion we become blood brothers of the Son of God, the King of Kings. This is heady! 'The Spirit himself beareth witness with our spirit, that we are the children of God: and if children then heirs; heirs of God, and joint-heirs with Christ (Rom. 8:16–17).

The Healing Serpent

There is a story of the time when the Children of Israel were camping in the wilderness (in Numbers 21). There was a great plague of serpents and they bit the people, who were dying like flies. Moses was told to take a brazen (brass) serpent and put it up on a pole, and anyone who looked on it would be healed. Jesus refers to this story and ties it to himself in John 3:14: 'As Moses lifted up the serpent in the wilderness, so must the Son of man be lifted up.' He knew that when he was 'lifted up' on the Cross, like the serpent on the pole, he would have power to give healing to others.

I don't know how this works, how the symbol of suffering brings strength. You might consider the snake in the light of homeopathic medicine and vaccination, where a small dose of the thing that causes the trouble can be a cure for it. The hair of the dog that bit you! Primitive people have believed that if eating a plant made you sick, then eating a little more of it might cure you.

Incidentally, the sign of the Medical Corps is serpents round a Cross. There is this ambiguous idea, that the serpent is an evil thing and yet somehow it takes part in healing. The idea of the serpent in the Bible is very rich in meaning. In the garden of Eden the serpent is evil; but when Moses' rod becomes a serpent and he grasps it – it takes courage to pick up a serpent! – it then becomes his rod by which he does the miracles (Exod. 4:4 and 10–17). By the same principle, Christ on the Cross becomes power, changing, transforming, transmuting evil into good. When he is lifted on the Cross, like the serpent, he brings healing. The Cross, which is the instrument of torture and death, becomes the instrument of life. Isaiah 45:22: 'Look unto me, and be ye saved, all the ends of the earth' – I see that as a prophecy of Christ as the serpent on the Cross.

I believe we cannot separate the agony of the world as we know it today from the agony of the Cross. They are inextricably bound together. The agony of the world is obvious: the famine and starvation, the massacres and the murders, the fighting and the fear, the discarded people, the destitute and the derelict, the murder squads and executions. Closer to us there is cancer; there are people born with horribly malformed and twisted bodies and there are mentally handicapped people. All of these are evidence of the agony of the world – the insoluble and the intolerable which distress us on every side.

I think the only thing for us to do is to set that agony of the world, those agonies, over against the agony of the Cross. I am not saying that it makes sense, but it seems to me to be our experience that it makes the best sense that there is. Solzhenitsyn writes about this – how the crucifix, seen or held, brings some strength to those in these impossible conditions. A number of the world's great sufferers have told how having a crucifix to look at or to hold somehow, in an extraordinary way, brings some light, or some comfort, or some strength, into the situation.

The Cross and the agony of the world are inextricably linked and entwined. The cry of agony is made up of many strands. There are screams, and there are whimpers from those who are too weak to scream. There are cries of pain, fear, despair, desperation, and of anger at the injustice of it all. The cries rise insistently and uninterruptedly from all the corners of the earth. There are many who cannot look to the Cross, so our prayers must lift up that cry. The Church through the world, day and night, lifts up its prayers to God. You, with your little mustard-seed of faith, must hold the world's pain up to God in unceasing intercession.

The Day of Atonement

Another Old Testament foreshadowing of the crucifixion is the Day of Atonement. This was the tenth day of the seventh month, the most important day of the Jewish year, when the sacrifice was offered for the sins of all the people of God.

In Leviticus 16 there is an account of the instructions given to Aaron the high priest for celebrating the rite in the wilderness. Two male goats were brought to the Tent of Meeting. Lots were cast to decide which should be the scapegoat and which should be the Lord's goat. The high priest put his hands over the head of the scapegoat – as the priest puts his hands over the oblations at the Eucharist – and confessed over it all the wickedness and rebelliousness and sins of Israel. He put the sins of Israel on to the goat which was then led off into the wilderness. The Lord's goat was slaughtered and offered to God as an act of atonement, to put relations right between God and his people.

In the days of the Temple this was a fearful and tremendous occasion. The high priest wore his vestments with golden bells on his skirts. He took the blood of atonement into the holiest part of the Temple, into the part which was never entered except by the high priest, and by him only once a year on this day of solemnity. He knew that the holy place was empty except for the massive, aweful, presence and glory of God. The bells on his vestments tinkled and he moved in a swirl of incense as he offered the life blood of the victim to atone for the sins of Israel.

In this rite there was a pattern and foreshadowing which pointed to an eternal reality. The scapegoat was led out into the wilderness as Christ was led out of the city. The Lord's goat was offered to God for the sins of the people as our Lord shed his blood for us. The high priest went into the holiest place, the holy of holies, as Christ entered heaven, the holy place, the holy of holies, as our great high priest. Read about that in Hebrews 9, where it is pointed out that the sacrificial life which Christ offers was given 'once, only once, and once for all'. 'Neither by the blood of goats and calves, but by his own blood he entered in once into the holy place, having obtained eternal redemption for us' (Heb. 9:12).

> For as the Priest of Aaron's line
>   Within the Holiest stood,
> And sprinkled all the mercy shrine
>   With sacrificial blood;
>
> So he who once atonement wrought,
>   Our priest of endless power,

> Presents himself for those he bought
> In that dark noontide hour.
>   (W. Bright, AMR 398)

And having returned to his Father in the holy place, there
'he ever lives to make intercession for us' (Heb. 7:25). We
commemorate that on Ascension Day when we begin our
service: 'We have a great high priest who has passed through
the heavens, Jesus the Son of God. Alleluia! (ASB, p. 627).

The Demands of Sacrifice

'God so loved the world that he gave his only begotten Son . . .'
(John 3:16). This great text is complemented by another: 'The
Father sent the Son to be the saviour of the world' (1 John
4.14). God so loved that he gave; loving and giving are insepar-
able, for love is expressed in giving; giving is love in action.
Throughout the Bible we are being shown what God gives to
his people; this is a central theme of the Old Testament and
the New Testament. We see how, in response, the people of
God were taught to make gifts to him. Through history they
learnt to make sacrifices as a way of giving things to God. Early
in Genesis we have the story of how Cain 'brought some of the
fruits of the soil as an offering to the Lord', and his brother
Abel brought 'some of the firstborn of his flock' (Gen. 4:3, 4).

As a pattern of sacrifices developed, three things emerged
which are significant for us as we look at the sacrifice of Christ
on the Cross.

First, anything to be sacrificed to God had to be perfect,
for example a lamb without blemish of the first year. This
foreshadows the belief in Jesus' birth of a pure virgin, and his
life and death without sin.

Second, a sacrifice had to be burned completely; it had to
be totally given and consumed. This is echoed in John 13:1:
Jesus 'having loved his own which were in the world, he loved
them unto the end' – to the end of his life, and to the limit of
his love, and to the total, utmost, oblation of the Cross.

Third, what the Jews gave to God in their sacrifices was the life of the victim. They did not think of offering dead animals; that would be no use at all. They gave the life of the animal, for they believed that the essence of the animal's life was in the blood. After the killing there was the blood-letting, and the blood was thrown on the altar or given to God in some symbolic way.

But the sacrificial system of the Old Testament comes to an end. The prophets thundered against the people who offered their sacrifices but failed to see what they meant. Isaiah, for one, taught that God had no use for their formal sacrifices:

> To what purpose is the multitude of your sacrifices unto me? saith the Lord: I am full of the burnt offerings of rams, and the fat of fed beasts; and I delight not in the blood of bullocks, or of lambs, or of he-goats . . . Cease to do evil; learn to do well; seek judgement, relieve the oppressed. (Isa. 1:11, 16, 17)

The sacrifices should have been a symbol to the people of a deeper kind of giving which God wanted. He wanted them to be willing and obedient and to give themselves by living according to his standards. It is not a sacrifice of our possessions which God demands but a sacrifice of ourselves – without blemish, without stain, without sin. The Old Testament comes to a juddering halt because that is precisely what man cannot give. And into that gap comes Jesus to give himself for us.

The Lamb without Blemish

The Jewish religion comes up against a wall, a chasm, a block. The religious man faces a black and hopeless situation, for he knows that he cannot give what God asks of him. He cannot offer himself as a perfect offering because he cannot live without sin. But into that gap, between what God demands and what a human being is able to give, comes Jesus, sent by his Father to be the Saviour of the world. 'Look,' says Jesus, 'It is all right. You cannot give a perfect life to God, but I can.

My life, my body and blood, are given on your behalf.' And because he is the Son of God, the life which he gives is infinitely valuable and eternally available.

Remember how at the Last Supper the phrase 'my blood which is shed for you' (Luke 22:20) brings together the blood shed in his Passion with the blood given to us in the communion cup. He shows his disciples his life blood given here in the upper room and about to be given there on the Cross.

Remember the central figure of the lamb in Old Testament sacrifices and the way in which, in John's Gospel, John the Baptist points out Jesus as the Lamb of God. 'Behold the lamb of God which taketh away the sin of the world' (John 1:29). Jesus said himself that he gave himself for other people: 'I lay down my life for the sheep . . . No one takes it from me, but I lay it down of my own accord' (John 10:15, 18).

In 1 Peter we are told that we were not redeemed with gold or silver 'but with the precious blood of Christ, a lamb without blemish or defect' (1 Pet. 1:19). He was 'tempted in every way, just as we are – yet without sin' (Heb. 4:15).

We read, 'He was chosen before the creation of the world, but revealed in these last times for your sake' (1 Pet. 1:20). He was totally given as 'he emptied himself and became obedient unto death, even the death of the Cross' (Phil. 2:7). He said himself, 'Greater love has no one than this, that he lay down his life for his friends . . . You are my friends . . .' (John 15:13–14). Our redemption through Christ's Cross was 'foreordained before the foundation of the world' (1 Pet. 1:20 AV). The Incarnation and Crucifixion were there in the mind and purpose of God before the creation. As he looked over the horizon and saw the sin of man, he planned how he might conquer its effects through Christ. Here on the Cross, God carried out his primordial plan, conceived before creation's 'big bang' – his own Big Bang!

The Water of Life

The Old Testament sacrifices underline the Jewish idea that blood was the stuff of life. The Old Testament also underlines the idea that water is the source and sustainer of life. The Jews remembered that they had emerged from Egypt by the waters of the Red Sea, and emerged into the Holy Land from the water of Jordan. And in the Holy Land they praised the Lord who 'sendeth the springs into the rivers which run among the hills . . . that he may bring food out of the earth, and wine that maketh glad the heart of men' (Ps. 104:10, 15). Water brings green growth to the golden burning desert. Water is always that which releases and sustains life.

Now consider the Cross as the source and sustenance of life itself. The death of Christ on the Cross releases his endless life into the world. The point is most clearly brought out by St John. John was the only one of the Twelve who witnessed the Crucifixion. All the rest forsook Jesus and fled, but John stood by the Cross, like the group of women who were also the first witnesses of the Resurrection and the empty tomb. John, the witness, records how a soldier with a spear stabbed Jesus' side. This was the common thing to do, the coup-de-grace. It is done today in evil regimes at mass executions; something may go wrong, so they put a bullet in each victim's head to make sure. The Roman soldier was trained in this, in the spear-thrust which made certain of death. 'One of the soldiers pierced Jesus' side with a spear, bringing a sudden flow of blood and water' (John 19:34 NIV).

The blood and water flowed at once; immediately he was stabbed 'forthwith came there out blood and water'. It was if they had been pent up inside the sacred heart and at the spear-thrust they are released. These words are rich in symbolism: they point us back to the Old Testament understanding of blood and water, and then forward to new Christian meanings.

Blood to the Jew was life. In their sacrifices they did not mean to give God a dead animal; they offered him the life which was released by the animal's death. So, we understand, it is with the Lord Christ, the Lamb of God; his death releases his life upon the earth. And as the psalmists and prophets saw water as God's supreme and life-giving gift, so we see water as the bringer and symbol of the life-giving power of the Cross.

And since the Son of God is eternal, the life and love which flows from him is eternal. Because he is infinite there is no stopping the flow: the precious blood and the living water will go streaming on to the end of time, flowing out to all the corners of the earth, on and on and out and out. There's that picture in Ezekiel 47:9: 'Every thing that liveth whithersoever the rivers shall come, shall live . . . every thing shall live whither the river cometh.' Wherever the river flows there is life.

Obviously the great sacraments are channels of Christ's life given to us in the water of baptism and in his blood which is the wine of the Eucharist. That goes without saying; those are the covenanted channels down through the history of the Church. But the river of life and love cannot be confined to those channels, and – thank God – it overflows them. It goes on and on and on, and out and beyond. You can't confine the life and the love of God.

The idea of Christ and his Cross as a fountain, or a stream, or the source of a river, is rooted in pictures to be found throughout the Bible. I will quote Zechariah. (I wish people could be persuaded to read some of what they call the 'minor prophets'; they are not minor, they are very important!) Zechariah says (13:1): 'In that day' – I think that means Good Friday – 'there shall be a fountain opened for sin and for uncleanness'; that is, a fountain to wash our sin and uncleanness away.

This idea of the water of life was specifically taken up by our Lord Jesus Christ himself in his own words. There is the lovely story from John 4 where Jesus sat by the well talking to the woman of Samaria. It was surprising in those days for a rabbi to talk in public to a woman, let alone a woman of Samaria. He said to the woman that he could give living water: 'Whosoever drinketh of the water that I shall give him shall never thirst; but the water that I shall give him shall be in him a well of water springing up into everlasting life' (John 4:14). There is his promise that he will be for us the water of life, giving us strong growth and refreshment.

Let us ask Jesus for his gift. 'Ho everyone that thirsteth, come ye to the water' – to Jesus – 'Come buy wine and milk without money and without price' (Isa. 55:1). 'The wilderness and the desert shall rejoice and blossom as the rose' (Isa. 35:1). And as water brings life into the desert, so into the desert of our lives, the emptiness and the muck we make of things, the living water of Jesus will be the source from which our life will grow and blossom.

2

The Song of Love

The more we read the Bible the more we find that the different writers echo or foreshadow each other. Our Lord's words grow in meaning as we see them in the light of Old Testament story and prophecy. The prophecy and poetry of the Old Testament grow in meaning as we find in it touches which read like allusions to events which, when the Old Testament was written, had not yet come about. Christians have often found that the historical meaning of Scripture does not exhaust its meaning for them. The imagery of the poetry and psalmody has spoken to the imagination in ways which help to interpret the work of Christ and to enrich our Christian experience.

The Canticle, or the Song of Songs – also known as the Song of Solomon – is a great love poem. Of course there are parallels between human love and divine love, and the poem has yielded different allegorical meanings to different ages. Jews have read it as a picture of the love of God for his people and Christians have read it as a picture of the love of Christ for the Church. I want to show you some of the insights which it suggests to me when I read it in the light of the love which brought Christ to the Cross and which we learn to know day by day through the Eucharist, through our prayers, and through trying to live as Christians.

The Song is a dialogue between the Bridegroom and the Bride, the Lover and his Beloved. I have generally quoted from the Revised Version because, though it keeps close to the poetry of the Authorized Version, it shows more clearly when the speaker is the Bridegroom or the Bride. Also, it is sometimes rather clearer than AV and, like most modern versions, it sets the poetry

*out in verse form. It sometimes helps to refer to the words which
different versions have used.*

Seeking our Lord

By night I sought him whom my soul loveth;
I sought him but I found him not,
I said, I will rise now, and go about the city,
in the streets and in the broad ways,
I will seek him whom my soul loveth:
I sought him but I found him not.
The watchmen that go about the city found me;
To whom I said, Saw ye him whom my soul loveth?

                                                    (Song 3:1–3)

On Good Friday we watch with Christ as he achieves the
greatest act of love in human history. What can the great
Canticle of Love suggest to us about this? Like all truly great
love poetry the Song has many moods. Basically it is of course
triumphal and rich with the joys of love, but it varies its music,
its tones, its moods. Besides its joy it also has shadows and
moments of darkness, as when the Bride thinks she has lost
her lover.

I do not believe that there is any real love which does not
involve darkness and suffering, for example the suffering of
loss and desolation. The darkness of his people's distress is
reflected in the physical darkness at the time of Christ's death.
'And when the sixth hour was come, there was darkness over
the whole land until the ninth hour' (Mark 15:33).

The bride who thought she had lost her lover had to find
him for, and by, herself. We too have to find Christ for
ourselves; others cannot find him for us. Our relationship with
him is personal and unique; other people cannot really show
him to us. In the garden, on Easter morning, Mary Magdalene
asked the 'gardener', 'Sir, if thou hast borne him hence, tell
me where thou hast laid him.' Then Jesus said, 'Mary,' and she
cried out, 'Rabboni!' – which means master or teacher (John

20:15, 16). When we picture that incident we sense the special personal relationship between them. We too have our special relationship with our Lord.

That close relationship is suggested when the groom in the Song calls his bride 'my sister, my spouse,' and gives her other loving names. He finds different ways of looking at their relationship – rather Jungian ways perhaps! So we have different ways of expressing our relationship with Christ. We may know people in a close family relationship, and this reflects one kind of relationship with Christ; we are our Lord's brothers born again as joint heirs with him. We may know another person, as lover and beloved know each other; our relationship with Christ is like that too. Then we may have a special relationship with people who inspire us, or teach us, or show us the meaning of things; we have also that kind of relationship with him.

We see Christ giving meaning to everything. We see him at the centre of the universe and the centre of our lives. It is no cliché to say that love is the central meaning of things, and the Cross is the final expression of love. The power of the Cross goes out as a healing force which absorbs and soaks up and cleans away evil.

> In the Cross of Christ I glory,
>   Towering o'er the wrecks of time;
> All the light of sacred story
>   Gathers round its head sublime.
>
> When the sun of bliss is beaming
>   Light and love upon my way,
> From the Cross the radiance streaming,
>   Adds more lustre to the day.
>   (EH 409)

The radiance which streams from the Cross is not so much light as healing rays, like radiation treatment which penetrates deep into the cancer of all the world's sin.

Sealed Together

The bridegroom speaks:

> Set me as a seal upon thine heart, as a seal upon thine arm:
> For love is strong as death . . .
> Many waters cannot quench love,
> Neither can the floods drown it . . .
>
> (Song 8:6, 7)

This is the seal which holds the lover and the beloved together in love. It is like the rather mysterious key of the great Advent antiphon, *O Clavis David*:

> O Key of David, and Sceptre of the house of Israel: that openest and no man shutteth, and shuttest and no man openeth: Come and bring the prisoner out of the prison-house, and him that sitteth in darkness and the shadow of death. (EH 734)

For many of us the antiphon may be more familiar as an Advent hymn. There is J. M. Neale's translation:

> O come, thou Key of David, come,
> And open wide our heavenly home;
> Make safe the way that leads on high,
> And close the path to misery. (AMR 51)

Or there is the eighteenth-century translation:

> O come, thou Lord of David's Key!
> The royal door fling wide and free;
> Safeguard for us the heavenward road,
> And bar the way to death's abode. (EH 8)

The origin of this lies in Isaiah: 'And the key of the house of David will I lay upon his shoulder; so he shall open, and none shall shut; and he shall shut, and none shall open' (Isa. 22:22).

In the antiphon Jesus is called a key. We may see the Incarnation as the locking together of God and man. In Christ, more specifically in his Cross, God and man are sealed together, locked together in love. The key of the Son of God was inserted into man via Mary at the annunciation, at his conception. The Cross marks the last excruciating twist which finally locks man and God together. The Cross is not just a thing, it is a mighty act of God in which that key is finally turned.

Christ always was God; he was begotten of the Father before all worlds. In a sense he became man progressively as he lived through conception, incubation, birth, youth and manhood. He was fully and finally identified with mankind only when the whole course had run, and he had shared death as well. God and man were inextricably locked together in the completion of the Incarnation.

At an even deeper level God and man were locked together at the Cross. Not only did Jesus share death there, but he shared the lowest depths which man may experience. He died disgraced and degraded, denied, betrayed, unjustly tried, scourged and naked. He died as the most desperate die, screaming for drink, feeling deserted by God, in doubt and despair. He shared the suffering of humanity at its worst. He shared our 'passion'. When that was done, he could know his task was accomplished and say, 'Tetelstei' – 'It is finished' (John 19:30). That was Christ's great freezing cry out of the darkness. And the veil of the Temple split from top to bottom.

'*Love is as strong as death*' – so one would think. Many poets have claimed it. But we have evidence that in fact love is infinitely stronger than death. Love is totally invincible. The factual evidence is the Resurrection and the fact of the empty tomb where the disciples found just Christ's graveclothes lying there flat. Nothing – not death, not the soldier's spear, not the solid rock, not the seal of Pontius Pilate – nothing could hold down love. Nothing can.

'*Many waters cannot quench love, Neither can the floods drown it*' – (or in NIV 'rivers cannot wash it away'). We may picture love as a great consuming fire which no water can put out. One of the Bible's first pictures of God is that of the burning bush which was shown to Moses. Though it burned and flamed 'yet the bush was not consumed' (Exod. 3:2). The fuel is eternal and cannot be spent. No floods can quench the flame of God's love.

Even the dark flood of our sin and the world's sin cannot douse that fire. Nor can it be put out by pain, or anxiety, or sorrow, or shame, or any of the questionings which flood our minds with scepticism or mistrust. We live in the midst of 'many waters'. We are tossed about – 'With many a conflict, many a doubt, Fightings and fears, within, without . . .'. But neither our personal, nor our national, nor our global afflictions or anguish can undermine or topple or demolish his love, which remains utterly stable. Our evidence is the way that Christ endured the Cross and afterwards rose again.

Drink Abundantly

The bridegroom speaks:

> I will get me to the mountain of myrrh,
> And to the hill of frankincense . . .
> I am come into my garden, my sister, my bride:
> I have gathered my myrrh with my spice;
> I have eaten my honeycomb with my honey;
> I have drunk my wine with my milk.
> Eat O friends;
> Drink, yea, drink abundantly, O beloved.
>   (Song 4:6; 5:1)

I have come into my garden.   The Bible's story of our salvation began in a garden. In Eden there were two trees, the tree of Knowledge of Good and Evil, and the Tree of Life (Gen. 2:9). It came to a crisis in a garden, in Gethsemane, where Jesus prayed, 'O my Father, if it be possible, let this cup pass from me: nevertheless not as I will, but as thou wilt' (Matt. 26:39). 'Now in the place where he was crucified there was a garden; and in the garden was a new sepulchre, wherein was never man yet laid. There laid they Jesus . . .' (John 19:41). And when Mary Magdalene sought for Jesus' body and saw him in the garden, she thought he was the gardener. We too seek in that garden, reaching out towards the Tree of Life. Eternal life is within our grasp here as it could not be in Eden.

I have drunk my wine with my milk. Milk is the drink of infancy and wine the drink of maturity. Christ's maturity was all of a piece with his childhood. The passion was a thread which ran through his life from beginning to end. The suffering of his death was all of a piece with his life and not just the culmination of it. Remember Simeon's words to Mary in the Temple: 'This child is set . . . for a sign which shall be spoken against; (yea, a sword shall pierce through thy own soul also)' (Luke 2:34–5). Compare the NEB translation: 'This child is destined to be a sign which men reject; and you too shall be pierced to the heart.' The rejection of Christ's message had brought him to the Cross, and no sword can have hurt his mother more than the soldier's spear which pierced her son's side.

I will get me to the mountain of myrrh, And to the hill of frankincense . . . I have gathered my myrrh with my spice. The gifts of the Magi at Jesus' birth link with the hill of Calvary. The myrrh points to the spices which the women brought to the grave in order to anoint his body. The 'hill of frankincense' points to the 'green hill far away'.

I have eaten my honeycomb with my honey. The spices remind us of the bitter pain of death; and yet in a sense Jesus' death was sweet. He endured the cross 'for the joy that was set before him' (Heb. 12:2). His joy lay in the knowledge of our salvation. His motivation was his love for us.

I can also think of Isaiah's words to King Ahaz which have often been read as a prophecy of Christ: 'Behold a virgin shall conceive, and bear a son, and shall call his name Immanuel. Butter and honey shall he eat . . .' (Isa. 7:14, 15) Whatever their original meaning, the words remind me of the sweetness of our Lord's joy.

Eat, O friends, Drink, yea, drink abundantly, O beloved. I read this as a great invitation to communion. Christ longs to eat and drink with us as he longed to feast with his disciples. 'And he said unto them, With desire I have desired to eat this passover with you . . .' (Luke 22:15). ('How I have longed to eat this Passover with you . . .!' NEB.)

Jesus came that we might have life and have it more abundantly (John 10:10). The Eucharist is the sustenance of our Christian life. It is our manna for our way through the wilderness, our rations for our pilgrimage. Remember the manna – 'It was like coriander seed, white; and the taste of it was like wafers made with honey' (Exod. 16:31). And it was only for the interim, for the journey. It would have no place in the promised land which would be flowing with milk and honey. So we look forward to another time in another place where we shall need no bread and wine, for we shall have full communion with our Lord.

In the meanwhile let us take his gifts 'abundantly'. Let us receive communion frequently. For some this means weekly and for some it means daily. For Christ invites us: 'Eat my friends . . . Drink abundantly, O Beloved.'

Upon the Mountains

The bride pictures the groom coming to her house to fetch her. Then he comes and calls her to come away with him.

> The voice of my beloved! behold, he cometh,
> Leaping upon the mountains, skipping upon the hills.
> My beloved is like a roe or a young hart:
> Behold, he standeth behind our wall,
> He looketh in at the windows,
> He sheweth himself through the lattice.
> My beloved spake and said unto me,
> Rise up, my love, my fair one, and come away.
>
> (Song 2:8–10)

We have already thought about the urgency, the longing of his love and desire for us which brings our Lord leaping, bounding, towards us. Now let us look at some of the mountains from which he leaps out to us. There are sacred, numinous, mountains all over the world, mountains of India and the East, Mount Fuji in Japan, Mount Athos of the Greeks; but think now of the mountains in the Bible.

Certainly one of the original holy mountains is Mount Sinai which the Bible also calls Horeb. There Moses saw the burning bush, and when he came there with the Children of Israel, 'Mount Sinai was altogether on a smoke' (Exod. 19:18). There, at Mount Sinai, God gave us the old covenant, the ten commandments. We are certain that he is present in the Old Testament as well as in the New Testament. The old covenant and the new covenant were both from him and both are covenants of love. We must seek him in both and we will find him in both.

There are other incidents which happened on mountains. Remember Elijah in his cave on Mount Carmel and how, after his strife with the prophets of Baal, he went to 'Horeb the mount of God', that is to say to Mount Sinai (1 Kings 19:8). And there he waited for God.

And, behold, the Lord passed by, and a great and strong wind rent the mountains, and brake in pieces the rocks before the Lord; but the Lord was not in the wind; and after the wind an earthquake; but the Lord was not in the earthquake: And after the earthquake a fire; but the Lord was not in the fire: and after the fire a still small voice. (19:11–12)

God spoke to him in a 'still small voice'. A modern translation puts it, 'And after the fire came a gentle whisper' (NIV). The Lord spoke with a quiet voice such as we may ourselves hear today.

Then there was the bright Mount of the Transfiguration, where Peter said to Jesus, 'Master, it is good for us to be here' (Luke 9:33). We know times when all is bright and glorious, when things go well and we are glad, like the disciples, to be with our Lord. Now we picture him at the dark mountain, the final mountain of Calvary-Golgotha. Here his disciples did not say 'Master, it is good for us to be here', for instead 'they all forsook him and fled' (Mark 14:50).

In the Song the beloved sees her lover behind the wall. This reminds me how Jesus suffered outside the Holy City:

> There is a green hill far away,
>> Without a city wall,
> Where the dear Lord was crucified,
>> Who died to save us all.

The Letter to the Hebrews reminds us of the ancient sacrifices which the Hebrews 'burned without the camp' (Lev. 4:12). 'Wherefore Jesus also suffered . . . without the gate' (Heb. 13:12–13). His death outside the city walls reminds us that he died as a sacrifice.

We may think of the walls which we build around ourselves. We try to hide from each other. We hide ourselves from ourselves. We build this wall to hide from our Lord, and yet we go on searching for him. Our search for our true selves may be one and the same as our search for our Lord; in finding him we may find ourselves. He 'shows himself through the lattice.' There are cracks in the walls which we build about ourselves. We try to hide. We may cover our eyes with the lattice of our fingers and just peep through the cracks. We are a bit ostrich-like; we pretend that he is not there. But he is there. He is seeking us everywhere.

Rise up my love my fair one, and come away.   Our Lord does not say 'Go away.' His constant invitation is 'Come with me.' He calls us to a solitude with him. 'Enter into thy closet and close the door' (Matt. 6:6). I picture the *poustinik*, the Russian-type hermit, in a bare room with a table and a Bible. We may meet him alone at a retreat. We may have our place of meeting at home. Even in the city we can shut off the business outside and make a place for solitude with him.

Kisses

Let him kiss me with the kisses of his mouth: for thy love is better than wine.   (Song 1:2)

In his book *True God* Kenneth Leech quotes an idea from some of the old mystics. They described three different stages of prayer as corresponding to the different stages of intimacy which different kisses suggest. The kisses of our Lord's feet are an expression of penitence. The kisses of the hands show a nearer relationship, when one comes to know Christ and serve him. The final stage of contemplation is like kissing the mouth in intimacy and adoration. I think it is quite a good description of the three areas of prayer.

The English are coy about kissing. Lest you think of talk of kisses as sloppy, I commend Psalm 85:10: 'Mercy and truth are met together: righteousness and peace have kissed each other.' The psalm continues about truth and righteousness flourishing on earth. It has to do with the coming of the Kingdom on earth with justice and liberty. The whole gospel proclaims liberation and the time 'that glory may dwell in our land' (Ps. 85:9). Kissing then may suggest to us the closeness of God and man in God's kingdom of righteousness and peace. Our prayer, 'Thy kingdom come', may pick up this vision in our intercession for the present United Kingdom in which we live, and where life is not always just and free.

There are three kisses in the gospels which we may link with our thoughts about the passion. There is the story – which is told a little differently in each of the four gospels – of a woman who anointed Jesus' feet with precious ointment. In Luke's account we read:

And, behold, a woman in the city, which was a sinner, when she knew that Jesus sat at meat in the Pharisee's house, brought an alabaster box of ointment, and stood at his feet behind him weeping, and began to wash his feet with tears, and did wipe them with the hairs of her head, and kissed his feet, and anointed them with the oil.   (Luke 7:37–8)

Luke sets the story in Galilee, earlier in Jesus' ministry, but the other gospels put the story of the woman's anointing in the last days in Jerusalem. (Compare this account with the others in Mark 14:3–9, Matthew 26:6–13 and John 12:1–8). Medieval churchmen sometimes ran the four accounts into one, as they sometimes ran Mary of Bethany and Mary Magdalene into one. Sometimes they assumed that Mary Magdalene was the woman in Luke's story, though there is no evidence of this. Yet in the Church's imagination she has often been seen as the sinner of whom Christ said that she had not ceased to kiss his feet and had washed them with her tears, and as the woman of whom he said that her story would be told 'wheresoever the gospel shall be preached throughout the whole world'. Whatever her name, there was a woman who kissed his feet and wept in penitence.

I wish I could repent like that. It is one thing to weep with remorse, to cry over spilt milk. It is quite another thing to have the gift of tears, to weep with sincere repentance.

Then there is Judas's kiss of betrayal (Mark 14:45). It shocked and surprised even Jesus. It was unbelievable. 'Judas, betrayest thou the Son of man with a kiss?' (Luke 22:48). That kiss was an absolute contrast to the woman's kiss of love and repentance. It was an absolute contrast to the affectionate touch of the woman who anointed Jesus with precious ointment which Christ had welcomed as a preparation for his burial.

Then, in Jesus' story of the Prodigal Son, when the son came home, the father 'fell on his neck and kissed him' (Luke 15:20). The kiss showed the father's acceptance of his son's repentance. Forgiveness was total and the son was reinstated: 'The father said to the servants, Bring forth the best robe, and put it on him; and put a ring on his hand, and shoes on his feet . . .' All of that acceptance is summed up in the kiss. It is a picture of how God our Father receives the penitent with redemption and reinstatement. It is a picture of the redemption which Christ wrought for us at Calvary.

The mystics who found in prayer an intimacy which they could describe as kissing Jesus on the mouth drew on an old conception of the kiss of life. You can trace the idea way back to Elisha breathing life back into the body of the dead boy (2 Kings 4:34).

> Breathe on me Breath of God,
>   Fill me with life anew,
> That I may love what thou dost love,
>   And do what thou wouldst do . . .
>
> Breathe on me Breath of God,
>   Till I am wholly thine;
> Until this earthly part of me
>   Glows with thy fire divine.
>   (E. Hatch, AMR 236)

'For thy love is better than wine' – let us look back to this passage we started from. Wine can be healing. Remember the Good Samaritan pouring oil and wine into the wounds of the man who had been set upon by thieves (Luke 10:34). But the love of Christ is better, more healing, than ordinary wine. Wine can also be heady and invigorating and we can understand this of the eucharistic wine. This is brought out in the translations of the prayer '*Anima Christi*': 'Blood of Christ refresh me', or even 'Blood of Christ inebriate me.'

In the Eucharist the kiss of peace is not just our kiss for our fellow Christians. The peace is given by Christ who made our peace with God on the Cross; it is his kiss. 'O Lamb of God that takest away the sins of the world, grant us thy peace.' I prefer the old rites which put the kiss of peace just after that petition because the peace which we share is granted to us by Christ, the Lamb of God. It is not primarily an act of reconciliation with each other but a receiving and giving of what Christ himself gives to us. The kiss of peace nowadays seems to be given at the offertory; I think the fact that the peace is derived from Christ is brought out better where the kiss follows the fraction, the breaking of the bread, just before the communion.

The Banqueting House

The bride speaks:

> He brought me to the banqueting house,
> and his banner over me was love.

Stay me with flagons, comfort me with apples:
for I am sick of love.   (Song 2:4–5 AV)

A modern version (NIV) makes the bride say, 'Strengthen me
with raisins, refresh me with apples, for I am faint with love.'

In the 'banqueting house' God and man meet. In the Old
Testament and in the New Testament we have images of the
king's feast, or the wedding feast, or the messianic feast which
inaugurates the kingdom of God. Jesus' parables suggest a feast
in which God and man come together, but to which we must
come with humility. Remember the story of the man without
a wedding garment.

We may think of Good Friday as a feast day, a day of
celebration. The first Good Friday was set in the context of the
feast of Passover, and that feast was a key to our understanding
of the whole Easter event. Similarly Good Friday is our day of
atonement, not the same as the Jewish Day of Atonement, but
sharing something of its solemnity and exaltation.

Christ's act of atonement is re-presented daily or weekly in
our celebration of the Eucharist. That is our banquet where
we feed on the 'bread of angels'. St Thomas Aquinas uses that
term in his great prayer of preparation for communion:

Almighty and everlasting God, behold I approach the Sacrament of Thy only-begotten Son, our Lord Jesus Christ. As
one sick, I come to the Physician of life: as unclean, to the
Fountain of mercy: as blind, to the Light of eternal splen-
dour: as needy, to the Lord of heaven and earth: as naked,
to the King of Glory: a lost sheep, to the Good Shepherd:
a fallen creature, to its creator: desolate, to the kind
Comforter: miserable, to the Pitier: guilty, to the Bestower
of pardon: sinful, to the Justifier: hardened, to the infuser
of grace. I implore therefore the abundance of Thine infinite
Majesty, that Thou wouldst vouchsafe to heal my sickness,
to wash my foulness, to enlighten my darkness, to enrich my
poverty, and to clothe my nakedness, that I may receive the
Bread of angels, the King of kings and Lord of lords, with
such reverence and fear, such contrition and love, such faith

and purity, such devotion and humility, as is expedient for
the welfare of my soul.

His banner over me was love. Banners bear the badges and
symbols of those whom they represent. Christ's badges are his
wounds in his hands and feet and side. They are his label and
the badges of his authenticity. When the risen Jesus came to
his disciples in the upper room, 'He showed them his hands
and his side' (John 20:20, 27).

> He bade them see his hands, his side,
> Where yet the glorious wounds abide;
> The tokens true which made it plain
> Their Lord indeed was risen again.
> (J. M. Neale, AMR 602)

It is the sight of Jesus' wounds which convinces Thomas:

> When Thomas first the tidings heard,
> How they had seen the risen Lord,
> He doubted the disciples' word.
>
> 'My pierced side, O Thomas, see;
> My hands, my feet I show to thee:
> Not faithless, but believing be.'
>
> No longer Thomas then denied;
> He saw the feet, the hands, the side;
> 'Thou art my Lord and God,' he cried.
> (Old Latin hymn, tr. J. M. Neale, EH 626)

Our hymns also picture the ascended Christ still bearing
'these dear tokens of his passion':

> See! he lifts his hands above;
> Alleluia!
> See he shows the prints of love;
> Alleluia!
> (C. Wesley, AMR 147)

This image of Christ seems to have been particularly dear to
Charles Wesley who uses it again in his Advent picture of our
Lord's return:

> Those dear tokens of his Passion
> Still his dazzling body bears,
> Cause of endless exultation
> To his ransomed worshippers:
> With what rapture
> Gaze we on those glorious scars!
>   (C. Wesley, AMR 51)

And we Christians should have our wounds to show if we are to have credibility and to be seen as authentic followers of our Master. There is little authenticity in a triumphalist church which does not suffer with the world.

His banner over me was love.   A canopy may be a protective covering, and the Cross is like a canopy of love which protects us. We may hide under it. And it is the flag of our allegiance in which we rejoice:

> In the cross of Christ I glory
> Towering o'er the wrecks of time . . .

Stay me with flagons, comfort me with apples.   The old AV translation pictures the juice of the grape rather than the cake of dried grapes, or raisins, which may have been in the writer's mind. I prefer the 'flagons' which suggest wine and signify for me the abundance of God's love and mercy. Remember the abundance of the wine at the marriage at Cana of Galilee when about 120 gallons of water were turned into wine!

While flagons of wine suggest times of celebration, apples are a contrast to this, for they are food of ordinary daily life. Our Lord will strengthen us through the common things; it is not always a time for rich exotic fruit like pomegranates and passion fruit.

The phrase 'comfort me' calls up the passage from Isaiah 40.

> Comfort ye, comfort ye my people, saith your God,
> Speak ye comfortably to Jerusalem, and cry unto her
>   that her warfare is accomplished,
>   that her iniquity is pardoned . . .

The NIV puts it nicely:

> Speak tenderly to Jerusalem, and proclaim to her
> That her hard service has been completed,
>   that her sin has been paid for . . .

We are reminded of the hard service which Jesus fulfilled on the Cross. Now our iniquity is pardoned; our sin has been paid for. Christ's purpose is accomplished. 'It is finished.'

I am sick with love.   We more generally think of being sick with sin. But let us pray that our sin may be pardoned and we may become infected with the love of Christ. We should pray that we may be so possessed and obsessed with love that we can only do loving things, that paralysis may grip us if we try to act otherwise! There is a prayer which I use after Communion which asks for that whole-hearted discipleship:

> Behold O Lord Jesus Christ, I now possess thee, who dost possess all things. Wherefore, my God and my all, I beseech thee to withdraw my heart from all things that are not of thee, in which there is naught but vanity and vexation of spirit. In thee alone let my heart be fixed, in thee let my repose be: where my treasure is, there may my heart be also.

Knocking at the Door

The bride speaks again:

> I was asleep, but my heart waketh.
> It is the voice of my beloved that knocketh, saying,
> Open to me, my sister, my love . . .   (Song 5:2)

I sleep but my heart waketh.   Compare Psalm 84:2, 'My soul hath a desire and longing to enter into the courts of the Lord.' I know that I often don't have any such desire! I am ready to sleep, and yet there is an underlying longing to be with my Lord. As Augustine put it, 'Our hearts are made for thee and are restless until they rest in thee.' While our bodies sleep our hearts and souls are awake to 'hunger and thirst for the living God.'

This has a practical application for those of us who find it hard
to sleep at night. We feel we ought to pray and yet we cannot
concentrate enough to do more than commend ourselves to
God and set our compass in his direction. If you are awake
enough to count sheep – don't count sheep! Count the wonders
of God's love for you, past and present and future. There is
an old mission hymn:

> Count your blessings, name them every one,
> And it will surprise you what the Lord hath done.

It is the voice of my beloved that knocketh. This is what Christ
is doing today and always. 'Behold I stand at the door and
knock' (Rev. 3:20). He goes on knocking, and you know it. 'If
any man hear my voice and open the door I will come in to
him.' It says 'any man', which of course means any woman too.
It means any sort of person – 'rich man, poor man, beggarman,
thief'. He came to the dying thief on the cross and he comes
to you and me. Christ does not ask just to come into the
hallway of our lives; he asks to come right in. We must not
treat our Lord as a visitor who comes knocking and stays for
a few minutes. Jesus comes to stay put! If you open the door
he will come in and make his abode with you. He will make
his home with you.

'Abide in me and I in you' (John 15:4). This sums up the
Christian life in its totality. The Christian life is nothing more,
nothing less. The answer which we must give when we hear
Christ's knock is in the penultimate verse of the Bible, the
climax of the whole Bible: 'Even so, come Lord Jesus!' (Rev.
22:20).

The bride hears her lover say, *Open to me, my sister, my
love.* Christ calls me 'my love' because I am his love. This is
not because I love him but because he loves me. In the book
of Daniel God's angel tells the prophet that he is greatly
beloved (Dan. 9:23; 10:8–19). These words to Daniel apply to
me too, for God loves us one by one. We are each unique –
the very hairs of our head are all numbered. We see the divine
love in the shepherd who went after one lost sheep, in the
woman who sought for one lost coin, and in the father who

welcomed back his one lost son. The Church has always taught that if I had been the only person to have existed Jesus would have died for me.

It is good to take the Cross as personally as one can. Remember, in Bunyan's *Pilgrim's Progress*, Christian's load dropped off and rolled away down hill when he came to the Cross.

Let Us Get Up

The bride is speaking again.

> I am my beloved's,
> And his desire is toward me.
> Come, my beloved, let us go forth into the field;
> Let us lodge in the villages,
> Let us get up early to the vineyards . . .
>
> (Song 7:10–12)

I am my beloved's.　I am his by creation. I am made by God for himself. Creation is not a thing of the past. He is always renewing and sustaining me, keeping me alive, giving life, health, consciousness, and awareness.

I am also his by redemption. I have been reclaimed and reinstated. Now redemption is a thing of the past; it was done on the Cross. Yes, but it is renewed day by day. As we fail him he is continually claiming us and reinstating us. Whether you are there or not, his pact with you is renewed every day at the Eucharist. 'This is my blood of the new covenant.' That is one of the points of priesthood, for the priest continually celebrates the Eucharist for the world, for the parishes, for you and me and all the people who are not there.

I commend you to 'get up early to the vineyards'! We do have midday Masses and evening Communions but I commend you to come early if you can.

> New every morning is the love
> Our wakening and uprising prove.

His desire is toward me.   This is the complement to 'my soul hath a desire and longing for him'. He has a desire for us which was expressed explicitly at the Last Supper at which the Eucharist was founded. 'With desire have I desired to eat this passover with you' (Luke 22:15); that is 'I have eagerly desired to eat this passover with you' (NIV). Not only at the end of his life does Christ show this desire towards us but as a youth, at his visit to the Temple, he said to his parents, 'I must be about my Father's business.' His Father's business was that of drawing us, of drawing me, to himself. In the Old Testament the picture of God as the Shepherd of Israel has the same idea, that the Father's business is to love and care for his people.

I think our Lord's desire is to share Communion with us at least every Sunday. But our desire is often to spend Sunday doing our own thing. We should come to him. We should respond, not out of duty or a sense of obligation, but as our love answers to his love.

Let us go forth into the field.   His voice calls us into the villages and the vineyards. We may understand this as his call to us to go out as apostles of his good news. 'Look on the fields, for they are white already to harvest' (John 4:35). 'The harvest truly is great, but the labourers are few: pray ye therefore the Lord of the harvest, that he would send forth labourers into his harvest' (Luke 10:2). We are the only labourers that God has and we should face the task, working with him in his labour of love. Let us gather in our sheaves, or even our one sheaf, if we can reach only one soul. Let us get out into the villages, into the churches, into the pubs, into the homes, into the streets of London, into villages by the Thames or the Zambezi, the Mississippi or the Indus – or wherever we live. Let us go out and proclaim the good news of Jesus and his love.

3

Looking and Listening

'When I survey the wondrous Cross,' I spend some time at Calvary, at the foot of the Cross. We must look and listen and think about what we see and hear. Preachers have often based their Good Friday talks on the Seven Words from the Cross. Our imaginations are furnished too from the images of the scene which painters and carvers and sculptors have given us down the years. Some paintings are fanciful or sentimental and others express the artist's real insights. Gonville has collected slides of pictures which he felt might help people to look at the crucifixion. We cannot print them here, but he sometimes refers to them in ways which may help us to look carefully at the pictures which we see elsewhere. Sometimes, he feels, there is more to be gained from looking at a picture in silence than from listening to an exposition. When we look at some detail or listen to some word we often find a simple personal application, and there are passages in this chapter which may help us to find our personal understanding.

Crucifixion

The gospels are stark: 'They crucified him.' Let us look for a moment at the actual process of crucifixion. I have a slide of an illustration from a book by Jean Vioulleaume. This shows the cross from the side and brings out the unnatural position into which the victim was stretched. The book gives a doctor's explanation of the strains to which the body was subjected and the way death came about. Here is another straightforward description from a school textbook.

> Crucifixion was a barbaric form of execution, though common enough in the Roman world, but there is little evidence on how it worked. It is probable that there were many variations on the basic method. Renaissance and Victorian depictions of Jesus' death show a lack of understanding of the way in which the human body is constructed: the palms of the hands, nailed, could not bear the weight of the victim and would tear through. It has been suggested that the arms were tied as well as nailed. It is more probable that the nail was hammered between the two large bones above the wrist. A piece of graffiti from the 1st century AD suggests that the victim stood on a small cross bar. The remains of the feet of a youth crucified about thirty years after the death of Jesus suggest that the ankles were sometimes nailed sideways to the cross and that a small platform was nailed to the upright to provide temporary relief from the weight on the arms, thus prolonging the suffering of the victim. These bones in the Museum of Israel in Jerusalem show that a second piece of wood, used in much the same way as a washer on a bolt, stopped the nail passing right through the ankle or the wrist. The pressure on the ribcage was enormous and death was often through suffocation. Sometimes the executioner would break the legs of the victim so that he would no longer be able to support the weight of his body and would thus quickly suffocate.   (Richard Hughes, *Belief*, OUP)

This grim description helps us to understand some of the different forms of crucifix which we may see. Charles Jagger's famous crucifix, which was made for the Society of the Sacred Mission at Kelham, shows Christ roped to the cross. There are many modern representations which show the nails driven through the wrists.

It is right to recognize the cruelty and pain of the Cross; but we should not brood and agonize over it without putting it in context, and trying to look through it to God's ultimate purpose. Many pictures are less concerned with the mechanics of crucifixion than with what the painter wants to say about it. They may emphasize the suffering or the glory. There is Graham Sutherland's twisted agonized Christ; there is Dali's picture in which the Cross hangs over the world. There is the strong face on the print of the Turin shroud.

The Russian Orthodox Church has a long tradition of icon painting. Icons are formalized religious pictures which do not aim at showing a realistic representation; they aim rather at presenting some theological truth, or some particular characteristic of our Lord. There are not many icons of the crucifixion, but there are some which – looking as from a heavenly vantage point – show Christ's passing being welcomed by angels. We can ask of every picture, realistic or full of symbolism, 'What special meaning has this picture for me?' We can always answer, 'This is an icon of God's love.'

Alone in the Crowd

I have an old picture of the crowd round about the Cross. It is a dark picture showing an amorphous milling mob. It suggests to me the first noisy excitement of the jeering people. 'He saved others; himself he cannot save. If he be the King of Israel, let him now come down from the cross, and we will believe him' (Matt. 27:42). If you are the Christ, come down – prove it! If he had come down it would have proved nothing; the people had already seen miracles. Now he has something else to show, that 'love is as strong as death'. A tide of hatred, contempt and indifference rolls in from the crowd, but 'many waters cannot quench love' (Song 8:7). Nothing can stop him from loving 'until the end' (John 13:1).

Picasso said, 'Painting is a blind man's profession. He paints not what he sees but what he tells himself about what he has seen.' As we tell ourselves about what we see at Calvary we create our own icons. We will not picture a crowd for long for, in a sense, there is no such thing as a crowd. Each person is an individual; each one of us, as an individual, is of concern to God. We cannot disclaim responsibility and hide from God in the crowd. Our icons will show something about how our personal lives relate to Christ's passion.

'When I survey the wondrous Cross' – it is noticeable how many of the hymns which we sing at this time have a devotional, personal tone.

> Glory be to Jesus,
>   Who in bitter pains,
> Poured for me the life blood
>   From his sacred veins.
>   (18th cent., tr. E. Caswall, EH 99)

The poet William Cowper (1731–1800) wrote:

> E'er since by faith I saw the stream
>   Thy flowing wounds supply,
> Redeeming love has been my theme
>   And shall be till I die.

Another eighteenth-century poet who showed a real joy in Christ's work was W. W. Shirley (1725–86):

> Sweet the moments rich in blessing,
>   Which before the Cross I stand,
> Life, and health, and peace possessing
>   From the sinner's dying friend!

Isaac Watts also points us to an overwhelming response:

> Were the whole realm of nature mine,
>   That were an offering far too small;
> Love so amazing, so divine,
>   Demands my soul, my life, my all.

Our own icons may be influenced by what we have read and sung, but we need some picture which we have made truly our own. We may be one of a crowd yet we meet his love each in our own way. We stand or kneel alone before the Cross.

Father, Forgive

> Two other men, both criminals, were also led out with him
> to be executed. When they came to the place called the
> Skull, there they crucified them, along with the criminals –
> one on his right, the other on his left. Jesus said, 'Father,
> forgive them, for they do not know what they are doing.'
> And they divided up his clothes by casting lots. (Luke
> 23:32–4 NIV)

Of course the soldiers did know what they were doing. They
knew they were hurting Jesus and they knew that they were
killing him. The nails that they had were not like our smooth
nails from a hardware shop or a DIY shop; they were rusty,
cast iron, and sharp. They were driven through the radio-carpal
nerve. The soldiers didn't particularly want to hurt him; they
'had to'. This is what people always say, for example, of our
treatment of non-whites in South Africa. (Well it's the way it
is. We have to do that. We must keep the *status quo* and our
white heritage.)

They didn't wholly realize what they were doing, and so
Jesus says, 'Father, forgive them.' Note that our Lord had the
power on earth to forgive sins which he had often demonstrated
(cf. Mark 2:5–10), but he does not forgive these sins for himself,
he asks the Father to do it for him. God is love. He does not
just love, he is love and that love cannot be changed. That is
the factual basis of the gospel. God knows what we are doing
for he has seen and experienced man at his worst – man who
crucifies – and he still goes on loving him. Christ has been
betrayed by his friend, his clothes have been torn off, he has
been scourged, he has been subjected to laughter and mockery
from men who think there is nothing funnier than a naked man
on show. He is taunted on the cross: 'If he be the King of
Israel, let him now come down from the cross, and we will
believe him' (Matt. 27:42). What else is left to be done? And
still he says, 'Father, forgive them.'

Jesus trusted his Father to forgive the soldiers. Why don't
you trust God to love you and forgive you? Why do you try to

bluff God, by showing him your good side, by pretending to be more religious than you are? He loves you whatever you do. 'I am not come to call the righteous but sinners' (Matt. 9:13). Why are we so anxious to be thought righteous? We pretend that we don't like sins. Of course we like sins or we wouldn't do them. What we need to do is to trust God and show him the truth about ourselves, to show him that we are selfish and fearful and proud.

We have all suffered from injustice, one way or another. We sometimes feel resentful or frustrated in our jobs and we tend to take it out on our families and those close to us. Why don't you take it out on God instead, because he can take it? Why don't you rage at him? We have seen things that we can't bear – like leukemia, and friends with cancer, and people born crippled and deformed. If you feel angry with God about those things, well, rail at him. He won't turn against you. He won't stop loving you. But you must be yourself not a pretend self. People say, with some truth, that reactive depression is re-pressed rage. Better not to repress your anger but to take it out on God. If you tell him how much you resent some of the things he has allowed to happen to you that is a step towards sincerity in your religion. Show yourself as you are and then his forgiveness can begin to pour into you.

They Kept Watch

> When they had crucified him, they divided up his clothes by casting lots. And sitting down, they kept watch over him there. (Matt. 27:35–6)

There is a picture by William Blake in the Fitzwilliam Museum in Cambridge which shows the soldiers gambling. The criminal's clothes were the soldiers' 'perks', and we see them gambling for the seamless robe – as we might toss up for something. What they were doing was negative rather than evil; gambling is not necessarily evil. But in this picture they are gambling behind the Cross, hidden from the crowd and from the eyes of

Jesus. They possibly preferred to be behind him so that they
didn't have to see what was taking place.

There are many people who prefer not to see reality. They
are absorbed in vice or absorbed in themselves and avoid the
real world with its suffering and evil. They try to contract out;
compare Pilate washing his hands. They are killing time, like
the gambling soldiers. They avoid today's crucifixions of war
and famine and the individual crucifixions of those facing guilt,
self-torment, bitterness, failure. They look away from the crises
of life and death. They act like children who feel that the horror
will go away if they do not look at it; they pretend that it isn't
there. They don't want to get involved in the troubles of this
world – for example, those of the Third World. But we are all
involved. It is no good trying to live in Cloud Cuckoo Land or
Never Never Land or just to fritter our lives away – for that
was just what the soldiers were doing, filling time, killing time,
fiddling while Rome burns. Horrors do not go away because
we cannot bear to look at them. Are there not very many
crucifixions going on in the world this day, at this moment, and
on a major scale? There is fighting and torture and famine.
There are men, women and children dying in depredation and
despair.

We must come out from behind and look at the Cross. We
must believe in the prayer which releases God's love and power
into the world. We must stand with agonized humanity and say
with and for the suffering, 'Lord, have mercy.'

We know that whatever men do to God or to each other
cannot destroy his love. The Crucifixion is the demonstration
of love persisting whatever men do.

The King's Throne

The inscription giving the charge against him read 'The King
of the Jews'. Two bandits were crucified with him one on his
right and the other on his left.   (Mark 15:26–7 NEB)

There are many pictures which show three crosses and on the

central cross, over Jesus' head, a notice is fixed. John's Gospel notes that the inscription was written in Hebrew, Latin, and Greek (John 19:20). Hebrew was the ancient language of the Jews' religious books. Greek had been spread round the Mediterranean and beyond by traders and conquering armies. Jews from abroad, in Jerusalem for the Passover, would understand it at least as well as their traditional Hebrew. Latin was the language of the Roman rulers. Jesus had said that if he was 'lifted up' (John 12:32) – meaning crucified – he would draw all men to himself. The title was set on the cross with irony by men who jeered at the claim that Jesus was a king; but the Christian finds in the words an unmeant recognition of his kingship, a statement of the truth. He is more than King of the Jews, he is King for us all.

The Christian also recognizes a foretaste of the outreach of Pentecost when, at the coming of the Holy Spirit, there were in Jerusalem 'devout Jews drawn from every nation under heaven' (Acts 2:5) who heard Peter and the rest preaching in the tongues they understood.

There is a picture in a children's Bible which shows Jesus close to; it shows the words on the title clearly and the different shaped letters used by the different languages. The picture also shows the head and shoulder of one of the thieves who were crucified with Christ. The presence of the convicted criminals at Christ's side drives home the double point: not only is Christ the King for all nations; he is the friend of all sorts and conditions of men. He wants 'publicans and sinners' in his Kingdom.

The thieves were rough tough men who could curse with the rest, but they were nearer to Jesus than the people in the crowd. They heard his prayer for the soldiers, 'Father, forgive them,' and one turned to him with his great request. Why one and not the other? Perhaps the other thief felt it would show weakness to recognize any good in Jesus. He was too proud for that. Why do we, or our friends, still refuse to turn to Jesus? It may be our pride, or our fear of showing weakness.

'Jesus, remember me', said thief, 'when you come into your kingdom' (Luke 23:42). Jesus' answer was 'quick and powerful'

(Heb. 4:12). 'Today', he said, 'you shall be with me in paradise.' The thief was the first of the redeemed, and he had done nothing to justify the free gift of God. He was the first-fruits of the Cross. He was the first citizen of the Kingdom where the first shall be last and the last shall be first.

This poem was copied from a parish magazine and we have not tracked its origin.

TO THE GOOD THIEF

It was naked and dirty that you saw him,
scourged and crowned with thorns;
nailed, a sack of bones outside the walls
on a pole – like a scarecrow.

And you, hanging on his right, you fellow
on his left, – writhing like skinned frogs
flea-bitten thieves – His retinue
courtiers to a mock king in his anguish.

REX JUDAEORUM: it was you first saw through the
    mockery,
You first saw the blasphemy as the living truth,
You who first believed the Latin, the Hebrew, and the
    Greek
And saw that the cross was God's throne.

O thief who stole paradise from the nails of a gibbet,
First gentleman of heaven,
pray for us at the hour of our death,
that we may see him and taste him.

(Based on a Welsh poem by Saunders Lewis)

There is a memorable prayer in E. Milner-White's *A Procession of Passion Prayers* which also sees Christ reigning from the Cross:

O Lord Jesus Christ, raised on thy throne of contempt and power, crowned with glory and thorns; Reign, O Saviour from the Tree over the whole world of sinful hearts, and over mine own; as thou reignest among the hosts of thy redeemed, God for ever and ever.

Remember Me

One of the criminals who hung there hurled insults at him: 'Aren't you the Christ? Save yourself and us!' But the other criminal rebuked him. 'Don't you fear God,' he said, 'since you are under the same sentence? We are punished justly, for we are getting what our deeds deserve. But this man has done nothing wrong.' Then he said, 'Jesus, remember me when you come into your kingdom.' Jesus answered him, 'I tell you the truth, today you will be with me in paradise.' (Luke 23:39–43 NIV)

The second word from the Cross is the quintessence of the pure unadulterated gospel. It is addressed to the dying thief who is crucified with him, a man who had done nothing to justify being saved. He was a social outcast who had lived on others and broken the law. He had taken part in the mockery of Christ himself and he knew that there was no hope for him and no good thing in him. Finally, he managed somehow to say, 'Lord remember me when you come into your kingdom.' And that's enough. He didn't have any faith – it was a purely selfish request, but it was a despairing reaching out to somebody. It is that that justifies him, not any good work he had done. 'Christ is become of no effect unto you, whosoever of you are justified by the law; ye are fallen from grace.' Perhaps a modern translation puts it a little more clearly – 'When you seek to be justified by way of law, your relation with Christ is completely severed: you have fallen out of the domain of God's grace' (Gal. 5:4 NEB). I wish I could make you see that. Too often you think you may go to heaven and have eternal life because of some good work or because of your good lives; but you cannot deserve heaven, you cannot earn heaven which is the gift of God. We must look to his grace. I think we should all try a little less and trust a lot more.

It is clear from the gospels and from this word from the Cross that Christ, the Good Shepherd, is where his sheep are. We need never be cut off from him. 'If I climb up into heaven, thou art there: If I go down to hell, thou art there also' (Ps.

139:7 BCP). He is with the dying thief in his hell, and he will be with you in yours. We get some hells in this life – loneliness, remorse, sin, and then we find Christ there. It is not a question of struggling to get out and then finding him; we find he is there in the depths with us. He is not to be found only where there is beauty and music and dignity; we may meet him in some beastliness and muck that we have got ourselves stuck in. 'Here I am,' says the Christ of the stable and the cross. Lord, have mercy on me, here in my sin. I am not cut off from him. I cannot be, even if the hell is one of my own making.

His promise was immediate, 'Today thou shalt be with me in paradise.' His promise is still that we shall be with him. Our prayer is still, 'Lord, Lord, remember me.' Lord, have mercy on me. He is there and nothing can separate us from the love of God – 'Neither death, nor life, . . . nor things present, nor things to come . . .' (Rom. 8:38). Yet there is one thing that can separate us from him, and that is trust in our own righteousness. That can separate us, but nothing else.

Behold Thy Mother

When Jesus saw his mother there, and the disciple whom he loved standing near by, he said to his mother, 'Dear woman, here is your son,' and to the disciple, 'Here is your mother.'   (John 19:26 NIV)

'Behold thy son. Behold thy mother.' In his third word from the cross Jesus commits to each other those two faithful ones who were at the cross, Mary his mother and John the beloved disciple.

Christ's way has been one of loneliness. He has fulfilled Isaiah's picture of the Servant – 'He is despised and rejected of men' (Isa. 53:3). As John's Gospel puts it, 'He came unto his own and his own received him not' (John 1:11). He is rejected by his own people, those whom he came to save. He is rejected by the nearest and the dearest, by Judas, one of the Twelve, by Peter who denied him. As for the disciples, after his arrest in Gethsemane, 'They all forsook him and fled' (Mark

14:50). Desertion and loneliness are integral parts of his passion. He had nobody to call his own, he had nobody to depend on. He is even losing his sense of his Father's presence.

Perhaps you have experienced loneliness like that – by bereavement, through a lover who leaves you, in sleeplessness, after failure. You have felt absolutely alone and thought, 'All I want is someone, anyone, whom I can trust and be with.' Personal relationships are utterly important to us and of course they were utterly important to Jesus.

This word is for us all. We are all being shown the need to relate with each other. We may find relationships difficult to handle. It is hard if we are one of those who hold desperately to others and cannot face life alone; we may make a nuisance of ourselves and be left more alone than ever. We may be among those who withdraw and who cannot make friends because they are afraid of being hurt and rejected. Most of us are a mixture of these types but we all need friends desperately.

'Woman, behold thy son. Son, behold thy mother.' How Mary and John needed each other! Perhaps there were very few left around the Cross when they dared come near enough to hear him and Jesus was able to commit those two to each other. He was saying to them what he says to us – 'You need each other. You can't just go on by being brave and praying.' You need relationships with each other which are deep and intimate. The Church is meant to provide the opportunity to make relationships; that is one of the things that the Church does. 'A new commandment give I unto you that ye love one another.' This is not just tea and buns. Nor is it the same as loving your neighbour, for in Christ Christians should love each other with the love which reflects the mutual love of the Father and the Son, and Jesus' love for his disciples. Our love should be the test of our sincerity – 'See how these Christians love each other.'

Unfortunately the sinful Church does not always provide the kind of fellowship or growing-togetherness which leads to love. Too often members of congregations do not love each other or even know each other enough to make the first steps. The Communion of Saints is meant to be a reality here on earth and not just the communion of the blessed in heaven. And this is the beginning of the Communion of Saints, our Lady and St John at the foot of the Cross.

I Thirst

> Later, knowing that all was now completed, and so that the Scripture would be fulfilled, Jesus said, 'I am thirsty.'   (John 19:28 NIV)

This is an almost unbelievable business. This is the man who promised living water. To the woman at Jacob's Well he promised, 'Whoever drinks the water I shall give him will never thirst' (John 4:13). And now he is reduced to this. No wonder the people mocked him.

But thanks be to God that there is nothing that our Lord has not suffered. He shares with the deprived and defenceless in their loss of almost everything. He had lost his clothes and his strength and his dignity. Now he has to ask his enemies for a drink. He knows the craving of thirst as an alcoholic knows it. There are times when a drink becomes an absolute necessity. It is like the drug addict's craving for a fix. That is the hell of our physical needs; our bodies cry out in pain or in lust, sometimes unbearably. Christ's understanding of these bodily needs is summed up in the words 'I thirst'.

There are times when one cannot pray. Sickness or worry or anxiety or fear or busyness may overwhelm us. There are times when you have just got to do the one thing in front of you: bear the pain, or do the job. Well, you must do it; you can't do more – you can't think of holy things. And Jesus had to go through the business of dying. 'I thirst.' He could not keep his mind on holy things or spiritual consolations. He was obsessed with his thirst, as we are sometimes obsessed with thirst, or lust, or envy. Preachers sometimes take the word symbolically and suggest that he was thirsty for the will of God, or thirsty for the souls of men, but for me that takes away some of the meaning, that he is able to sympathize with us in our deepest distress and agony.

There is always a danger of thinking of Jesus as a strange unnatural being. He wasn't. He was, and is, a man. He was, and is, also God, but that did not affect his manhood. He was 'tempted in every way, just as we are' (Heb. 4:15). At the Last Supper he called his disciples those who had stood by him in his temptations (Luke 22:28). He was and is a man, but a man as man was meant to be, that is without sin. Though he was perfect man he was still a human being, subject to the human conditions of suffering and evil. His suffering did not diminish him; nor need suffering diminish us. We are diminished by sin; we are deformed by it. The nature of man is that he is body, soul and spirit, and the spirit can't escape out of the body. Our bodies do matter, and so Christ's body mattered to him. All this I derive from the cry, 'I thirst'.

God-forsaken

And at the ninth hour Jesus cried out in a loud voice, 'Eloi, Eloi, *lama sabachthani*?' – which means, 'My God, my God, why have you forsaken me?'   (Mark 15:34 NIV)

Jesus knew what it meant to be deserted and betrayed and denied by his family and his friends. Now he feels that he has been deserted and betrayed by God himself. Was Christ deserted? The fact is that God, being who and what he is, could not forsake or fail Jesus. God is love, steadfast, unchangeable, unshakeable love. But though God had not withdrawn his love Jesus clearly felt as if he had.

This sense that God is not with us is a very real experience for many people. Think of the sense of god-forsakenness felt by millions in prisons or concentration camps, by refugees, by people faced with napalm bombing, by those who scream out against their lot – Why? Why this? Why us? And we in our lesser ways may know the reality of feeling utterly in the depths, surrounded by demons and devils of lust or fear or depression, down in the depths of our own hells. (Though we know that 'If I go down to hell thou art there also' 'Ps. 139:7 BCP). There is a state which psychologists call 'separation anxiety'; that is a part of it. There are long lonely weekends when people reach the lowest point of the human spirit, the point in which they may turn to suicide.

This moment on the Cross was a lower point for Jesus than his hour of agony in the garden, when 'he began to be deeply distressed and troubled' and said to the disciples who were with him, 'My soul is overwhelmed with sorrow to the point of death.' That was the great crisis of commitment when he prayed, 'Abba, Father, take this cup from me' (Mark 14:32–6). He told God that he could not bear it. He felt as we feel when we face fear of the unknown and the dread that something horrible and unbearable is going to happen to us. No, no, not that, whatever else you do, Lord! Not cancer, I don't want that! Not the death of my beloved! Not an old people's home, anything but not that! We have to face fears all our lives in lesser ways, fear of facing the world, fear of failure, fear of laughter, fear of being hurt; and fear of death, which is like all our other fears put together.

Yet despite his terror our Lord committed himself to God – 'Yet not what I will, but what you will.' Now on the cross he feels that God has let him down. We can imagine him saying to God, the Father, 'I committed myself to you, and look what happens.' The cup he was drinking was horrible, terrible, and he was drinking it to the dregs. But, thanks be to God, we know that his Father was in fact with him. We know that from history, from the resurrection. That feeling of dereliction and desertion and utter hopelessness was completely real to him; but the desertion was not objectively real for 'underneath there are the everlasting arms' (Deut. 33:27).

It Is Finished

A jar of wine vinegar was there, so they soaked a sponge in it, put the sponge on a stalk of the hyssop plant and lifted it to Jesus' lips. When he had received the drink, Jesus said,

'It is finished.' With that he bowed his head and gave up his spirit.   (John 19:29–30 NIV)

And when Jesus had cried out again in a loud voice, he gave up his spirit.
At that moment the curtain of the temple was torn in two from top to bottom. The earth shook and the rocks split.   (Matt. 27:50–1 NIV)

'It is finished.' These are the words recorded by St John, while in Luke's Gospel Jesus' final words are: 'Into thy hands I commit my spirit.' Before that quiet word our Lord cried with a loud shout. This is the crisis moment of the crisis in the history of our salvation. Our Lord cries out in triumph, 'Tetelestai' – it is done, it is finished, it is completed. The new way of redemption is opened for us. The M25 motorway was finished when it was ready for use; so the new road between God and man is finished and ready for use. And at this moment St Matthew reports, 'the curtain of the Temple was torn in two from top to bottom. The earth shook and the rocks split.' This marked the opening of the new highway:

> It will be called the Way of Holiness.
> The unclean will not journey on it;
> it will be for those who walk in that Way;
> wicked fools will not go about on it . . .
> But only the redeemed will walk there.
> (Isa. 35:8, 9 NIV)

And when the centurion and those who were guarding Jesus saw the earthquake and all that had happened they were frightened and exclaimed, 'Surely he was the Son of God!' (Matt. 27:54 NIV).

That is the main message, but there is another sense in which we may look at the phrase 'It is finished.' Most of us, at some time in our lives, have come to the end of our tether. We say 'I'm finished. I've had it. There is nothing more that I can do and I don't care what happens now.' You may be exhausted with battling and trying over your marriage, or over your children who have not turned out as you hoped, or over your job,

trying to please an impossible boss, trying to make ends meet
when they won't meet, trying to pull oneself together in a
period of migraine or depression. You say, 'I've had it! I'm
finished!' It would be good if you really meant that! The recognition of your own failure is not the beginning of the end; it's
the end of the beginning. Where you have come to the end of
your tether, that is where God begins. Give up. God can't run
your life while you think you are competent and can run it
yourself. If you really give up, Jesus can enter in. 'Come unto
me all that travail and are heavy laden and I will give you rest'
(Matt. 11:28 BCP). Rest, shalom, is a great Bible word. 'There
remaineth a rest unto the people of God' (Heb. 4:9). 'They' –
outsiders – 'shall not enter into my rest' (Ps. 95:11; Heb. 3:11).
They cannot enter into 'my rest', into the peace that Jesus gives
to us, unless they themselves give up the struggle, leave it to
God.

Jesus 'bowed his head and gave up his spirit.' The drama of
Calvary is over. Despite the noise and the violence our thoughts
have turned to Christ's peace and our peace. Is this stillness
an end? 'Only silence and some secondhand clothes' (Tom
Stoppard).

Into Your Hands

Jesus called out with a loud voice, 'Father into your hands I
commit my spirit.'   (Luke 23:46 NIV)

After chaos and violence of the crucifixion, after the terrible,
terrifying cry, 'Why hast thou forsaken me?', comes peace.

Christ is at peace. He is entering the peace which has been
obtained for us all, the peace with God with whom we are
reconciled. 'For God was pleased . . . through him to reconcile
to himself all things, whether things on earth or things in
heaven, by making peace through his blood, shed on the cross'
(Col. 1:20). This is the redemption of the whole creation. (Even
the fallen angels?)

Peace was one of the themes Jesus spoke about at the Last

Supper, so close before the Crucifixion. He made this promise to his disciples, 'Peace I leave with you; my peace I give to you. I do not give as the world gives' (John 14:27). 'I have told you these things, so that in me you may have peace' (John 16:33). And after the Crucifixion, when he came to the disciples on the resurrection night, he showed his hands and his feet and his first words were, 'Peace be with you!'

That is what he had set out to do – to bring the peace of reconciliation – and he had achieved it on the Cross. He had achieved peace with God for his disciples – and for you and me.

I don't think we lay hold of his gift or claim it enough: I don't think we seek it in enough depth. 'Let the peace of Christ rule in your hearts' (Col. 3:15). Do you? Do you let his peace take control over your anxieties and fears? Do you allow his peace to pervade you, to penetrate, permeate, saturate, and infuse you, to soak into your pores and into your bones?

The peace process begins for us in prayer. There we are absorbing the peace of God; that is one reason why prayer cannot be hurried. Indeed, hurried prayer is not really prayer at all. In quiet prayer we begin to forge a solid deep, interior base which cannot be shaken though winds and storms pound it and bang it and beat around it.

Then you must go on from that interior peace to show its fruits in your life in the external world. 'And live a life of love, just as Christ loved us and gave himself up for us as a fragrant offering and sacrifice to God' (Eph. 5:2). Live steadfastly, day by day, in love, clothed in love, and surrounded by love. Beloved, live lovingly and lovably in the peace of Christ.

4

Behind the Scenes

We have looked at what happened at Calvary on the first Good Friday. Now we turn to those events which we could not have seen with our eyes or heard with our ears. What was Christ doing on the Cross which transected time and rang the bells of heaven? Here are some tentative answers to that unanswerable question. Some readers may find this chapter the kernel of the book.

The Dark Glory

There are moments in the Old Testament when we sense God's glory. Let us remember Isaiah's description of his vision in the temple at Jerusalem in the year 742 BC.

> In the year that King Uzziah died I saw the Lord sitting
>   upon a throne, high and lifted up, and his train filled
>   the temple.
> Above it stood the seraphims; each one had six wings; with
>   twain he covered his face, and with twain he covered
>   his feet, and with twain he did fly.
> And one cried unto another and said, Holy, holy, holy, is
>   the Lord of hosts: the whole earth is full of his glory.
> And the posts of the door moved at the voice of him that
>   cried, and the house was filled with smoke.
>
> (Isa. 6:1–4)

Uzziah had been a strong king who had ruled on the throne of David for fifty-two years. The kingdom of Judah had prospered, but his death was to bring forward the breakdown of the kingdom under the rule of his weak sons and the threat from the great empires of Assyria and Babylon. The world of Judah, the world of Isaiah, was to fall apart. But God revealed himself. Despite the pending gloom of the national situation Isaiah was to look though the dark uncertainty and see the holiness of God.

The Crucifixion also came at a time of national darkness when the Jews were fearful under the heel of their Roman rulers and felt that their world was falling apart. Good Friday brought darkness and sorrow to the disciples whose world seemed in pieces. Though we sense this darkness we can look behind it and see the backcloth which Isaiah saw. Behind the horror of the Cross shines the tremendous, transcendent beauty of God who is present even in the horror.

We see our Lord 'high and lifted up', but in a different guise. St John's gospel shows Jesus foreseeing his crucifixion. 'As Moses lifted up the serpent in the wilderness, even so must the Son of man be lifted up' (John 3:14). Jesus saw the brazen serpent which Moses raised in the wilderness (Num. 21) as a symbol of the truth that his death would have power to give life to others.

Isaiah saw God in glory, but when Jesus was lifted up on the Cross there was no visible beauty in the scene. In Isaiah 52 and 53 we have a prophetic foreshadowing of the Suffering Servant of God – 'His visage was so marred more than any man . . . he hath no form nor comeliness . . . there is no beauty that we should desire him.'

The glory of the Cross is a dark glory. It is different from the bright dazzling glory of the Transfiguration. The Greek word *doxa* suggests a gleaming glory; so does the Jewish word for the light of God's presence, *shekinah*. But the Old Testament word for glory, *kabhod*, has a sense of weight and gravity and huge power which I think is possibly nearer to what I call the dark glory of the Cross.

Our eyes must get accustomed to the darkness of the crucifixion before we can see the beauty of the glory beyond it. But we are looking at the same Lord as Isaiah saw in the temple.

The angels still cry, 'Holy, holy, holy, is the Lord God of hosts: the whole earth is full of his glory.'

Enabling Reconciliation

I want to suggest some different answers to the question: What was Christ doing? What was he achieving there on the Cross? While we realize that it remains a mystery, we can feel our way round that mystery and find a little of its meaning.

First, 'God was in Christ reconciling the world to himself' (2 Cor. 5:19). His action was not confined to Christians, to members of his Church. God is concerned for the whole world, for his whole creation. Remember 'God so loved the world, that he gave his only begotten son . . .' (John 3:16). That is a central verse, so important that many Bibles underline it or print it in red. And 'Christ died for the ungodly' – that lets in you and me! – 'While we were yet sinners Christ died for us' (Rom. 5:6–8). His death was for us all, as he was 'the true Light that lighteth every man that cometh into the world' (John 1:9).

Reconciliation is usually a process in which two parties are drawn together. Both parties reach an agreement which is acceptable to both. Thus ACAS may be called in to reconcile employers and employees when they cannot agree on a wage settlement. There may have to be an element of give and take on both sides before agreement is reached. Both sides modify their position. But Christ's death certainly does not make God change his position. God's love for us remains steadfast; he does not change. With him there is 'no variableness or shadow cast by his turning' (Jas. 1:17). It is we who must change. It is we who need to change that we may be reconciled with God. And Jesus in his death is bringing that change about; he is making it possible.

God's love is steadfast. Christ's death on the Cross manifests this. It is the final demonstration of the length to which his love will go. We see there is no end at all to the love which Christ showed in his death and continues to show beyond death.

'Having loved his own which were in the world he loved them unto the end' (John 13:1). Here, as often in John's Gospel, we have a phrase which is true in more senses than one. Christ loved 'unto the end' in that he loved to the uttermost and gave his all. He loved 'unto the end' of his life. And beyond his death and resurrection he continues to love 'unto the end', for his intercession for us goes on. Here or yonder there is no end to his love.

Completing the Incarnation

What is Christ achieving there on the cross? He is completing the Incarnation by completing his total identification as a man among men. Perhaps the creation of man himself, *homo sapiens*, was as a step towards God's redemption of all creation, so that, through the Incarnation of Christ, he could be the means for reconciling the whole creation that groaneth and travaileth together until now (Rom. 8:22). Man is the peak of creation and Christ is the peak of man.

The Incarnation is the basic fact of our faith. John's Gospel tells us that 'the Word was made flesh and dwelt amongst us' (John 1:14). The Nicene Creed pronounces our belief 'in one Lord Jesus Christ, the only begotten Son of God, Begotten of his Father before all worlds, God of God, Light of Light, Very God of very God . . . Who for us men and our salvation came down from heaven, And was incarnate by the Holy Ghost of the Virgin Mary, And was made man.'

He was made flesh at the Annunciation. At Mary's moment of conception when – 'by the power of the Holy Spirit he became incarnate of the Virgin Mary . . .' (ASB) He was born as a baby at Christmas. He lived the life of a man but was only finally made complete man when he died as a man on the Cross. Then he had shared with us the last essential, inevitable, experience of human existence – death. His identification with man was total. Before his death he spoke his last words to us: 'It is finished.' But it was not just a human life that was finished: it was the Incarnation that was finished. It had been completed.

The Incarnation was finished as an action in time and place. The Son of God no longer dwelt on earth in human flesh. But manhood and godhead had been finally and indissolubly interlocked together there on the Cross. The Athanasian Creed speaks of 'taking the manhood into God'. The conception is a mind-boggling, mind-blowing mystery. Christ's divine nature lifts up our human nature into God. One of the Ascension Day hymns, looking forward beyond Good Friday, tries, in its picture language, to express this almost inexpressible truth:

> He has raised our human nature
>   On the clouds to God's right hand;
> There we sit in heavenly places,
>   There with him in glory stand:
> Jesus reigns, adored by angels;
>   Man with God is on the throne;
> Mighty Lord in thine Ascension
>   We by faith behold our own.
>   (Christopher Wordsworth, AMR 148)

What we cannot clearly grasp in an intellectual way we can grope towards in poetry. We can apprehend it without fully comprehending it. We take in the mystery in our prayers, with wonder and love, when – as the Eastern Orthodox put it – we take our heads into our hearts.

In order to obtain this total identification, to get right down to our deepest level, there had to be a total act of humility, of self-giving, by God in Christ.

Christ Jesus . . . though he was in the form of God, did not count equality with God a thing to be grasped, but emptied himself, taking the form of a servant, being born in the likeness of men. And being found in human form he humbled himself and became obedient unto death, even death on a Cross. (Phil. 2:6–8 RSV)

Note he 'emptied' himself, from the Greek *kenosis*. He did not empty himself of his divine nature, of himself, but he put aside the attributes of divinity, the manifestations of his glory, his majesty, and power, 'and became obedient unto death, even the death of the cross'. He emptied himself completely, down to the dregs, on the Cross. He faced the human experiences of fear, pain, and dereliction, and the depths of death itself.

There is an extraordinary verse: 'He was made to be sin on our behalf' (2 Cor. 5:21). I think it means that he experienced the effects which follow from sin – the sense of being cut off and forsaken by God. He identified himself with man even in sharing those consequences of sin.

So he completes Incarnation. 'It is finished.' Yet his death is not primarily an ending. We may say of a bridge that it is finished, meaning that it is open and ready for use. We may say of a road that it is finished; it is now in use. Jesus is opening the way to a new life. He is inaugurating the new creation, the new era, the new dispensation. Christ's death on the cross inaugurates the Kingdom and the new road to redemption.

Inaugurating the New Creation

What is Christ doing there on the cross? Good Friday is the first day of the new creation. This is its inauguration. The ending of Jesus' earthly life brings in the beginning of the new dispensation. Christ was inaugurating the Kingdom, not just completing his mission and purpose. When a bridge is finished and opened it is just beginning its useful life, which will end only when there is no further need for it. So the finishing of Jesus' earthly life marks the beginning of a new age which will be completed only at the Second Coming.

Here on the Cross we witness the birth of our new creation. What we see in the twisted agonizing death pangs of Jesus is in fact the birth pangs of a new creation. The similarity between birth pangs and death pangs is illustrated by the butterfly. It emerges from its chrysalis, struggling and writhing. It looks as if it is dying. It emerges but appears dead and inert; but in a short time it takes off in beauty. So, on the resurrection morning, Christ arises in beauty from the chrysalis of the Cross. There is a hint here that the trauma of human death may be the gateway to beauty. But at the Cross there is no beauty yet.

We may compare the story of the first creation in Genesis
and the second creation here. 'In the beginning . . . God said,
Let there be light: and there was light' (Gen. 1:3). We are
taken through the days of creation when the physical world is
called into being, then on the sixth day man is created. Creation
is finished – 'And God saw everything that he had made, and,
behold, it was very good . . . And on the seventh day God
ended his work which he had made; and he rested on the
seventh day . . .' (Gen. 1:31; 2:2). He rested on the seventh
day, the Sabbath, Saturday. So at the new creation which opens
the era of a new creature, a new man, the creative action of
Good Friday is followed by rest. Then he rested in the tomb
on the seventh day. On the first day of the week, Easter Day,
God's message is that of the first day of creation: 'Let there be
light.' The Light of the world arises.

The first creation was a smooth ordered outpouring of love.
God's love was the material out of which life was created. We
hear of the 'big bang' theory of the creation; perhaps the biggest
bang is the new creation at the Crucifixion. The second creation
is born of human material which has been twisted and flawed
by human sins. The violence of its birthpangs marks God's
work to untwist what is twisted and unscrew what has been
screwed up. Graham Sutherland's strained and twisted crucifix
in Northampton parish church expresses this idea of the trauma
of the new creation.

The sense that this new creation is God's own work stands
out in the Crucifixion story. God is in command, as when Jesus
says to Pilate, 'You would have no power if it had not been
given you from above' (John 19:11). Pilate is not fully responsible for his action for God is behind it; what he is doing is in
a sense being done to him. Christ's hour has come and the
minor characters must play their parts.

Here is another thought about this new creation. Consider
the Cross as the turning point in the process of evolution.
The basic instinct, self-preservation, enabled evolution and the
preservation of the species. Because of this instinct, acting
through aeons of ages, we came to be born. The sex instinct is
part of self-preservation and perpetuation. Born with this

instinct of self-preservation we are born with selfishness as a basic factor. Now, on the Cross, Christ reverses this process. He demonstrates that the way of self-preservation leads eventually to death while Christ's self-sacrifice, his death, opens the way to life – real life – eternal life. 'I tell you the truth, unless a grain of wheat falls to the ground and dies, it remains only a single seed. But if it dies it produces many seeds' (John 12:24). Christ's eternal life is a whole new ball-game, a new creation in which self-preservation does not apply, in which self-sacrifice takes its place. Therefore Jesus said, 'Ye must be born again' (John 3:3) – into this reversed process.

Of course we are still also part of the old creation. 'The flesh lusteth against the spirit and the spirit against the flesh.' That is, 'the sinful nature desires what is contrary to the Spirit, and the Spirit what is contrary to the sinful nature' (Gal. 5:17 NIV). Because our weak nature draws back from the way Jesus has pointed, therefore we have prayer and the sacraments to ensure the eventual triumph of the Spirit in us. We live in hope. 'Thanks be to God! He gives us the victory through our Lord Jesus Christ' (1 Cor. 15:57).

Breaking the Entail

Compare the symbols of the three great world religions. The Jews have the star of David and Islam the crescent moon. We Christians are more down to earth. Our main symbol is the Cross, the symbol of death, not the empty tomb, which might be thought of as the symbol of resurrection. Rather we emphasize the seal and sign of what was done on the Cross. The Cross is the mark of the precise spot in time and place, of the where and when of our salvation. That was where Christ's work was accomplished.

What was Christ doing on the cross? Another way of looking at the Cross is to see it as a point where our religion breaks sharply apart from the other religions of the world. What most other religions have in common is their belief in destiny, in the absolute inevitability of things. We see this belief in inevitability from Copernicus to Darwin, Marx and Freud. They assume a mechanical process. This is a basic human belief, which is only relieved by our concepts of the fatherly will of God and of the power of prayer to alter things and break through some pattern of fate or predetermination. This the opposite of the horoscope idea that the stars determine our future. Most people believe that somewhere there is a bullet with their number on it. That's the common human belief. It is played on by Hinduism, Buddhism, Zoroastrianism. They believe in Karma, or the endless wheel of destiny, or reincarnation until Nirvana and nothingness. The Muslim submits to the inevitable; he says, 'Kismet – it is ordained.' In all these religions there is belief in a chain of destiny or a wheel of fate which grinds inexorably on and on.

But we who are Christians do not believe in inevitability or inexorability, because we believe that God has intervened in history. The Incarnation is an intervention, and Christ on the Cross breaks the chain of sin and destiny. The Cross breaks the chain and releases us. It is the sign of our freedom. And Christ continues to intervene. 'It is Christ that died, yea rather, that is risen again, who is even at the right hand of God, who also maketh intercession for us' (Rom. 8:34). He intervenes in our lives, often at our invitation. Sins can be forgiven, and we can be saved and set free.

The Cross is the sign of freedom and of Christ's invitation to us. Through the Old Testament we hear God pleading to Israel. In the New Testament the invitation seems more personal: 'Come unto me all ye that labour and are heavy laden . . .' (Matt. 11:28). 'Behold I stand at the door and knock. If any man hear my voice, and open the door, I will come in to him, and will sup with him, and he with me' (Rev. 3:20). And the words of our answer are provided and set down for us in the Bible's last verse but one: 'Even so, come Lord Jesus' (Rev. 22:20).

Giving Himself

God gave us – he gives us – himself, and the climax of his giving is here on the Cross. He gives his life, which is himself.

We all have needs. I can't feed myself. I need farmers and I need transport workers; and those who are not vegetarians need butchers and fishermen. I can't keep myself warm without coal, gas or electricity. For my health I need doctors, dentists, nurses and pharmacists. For all these absolutely basic needs we are totally dependent on each other. Even more basically, I need people, persons to love and to love me. And I need to find a purpose in life, a direction. And of course ultimately my need is for God.

I need God first as my creator and then as my sustainer; but, deeper, and largely beyond my understanding, there is the need for God himself. We need God himself in his beauty and his wonder and his love. All through our lives he showers us with gifts, but ultimately we do not want God for what he gives but for himself. 'God so loved the world that he gave his one and only Son, that whoever believes in him shall not perish but have eternal life' (John 3:16). He gave his Son who is 'God of God, Light of Light, Very God of very God' (Nicene Creed).

Christ gave himself willingly. He emphasizes the point: 'I lay down my life . . . No man taketh it from me, but I lay it down of my own accord' (John 10:18). 'The good shepherd', he says, 'lays down his life for the sheep . . . and I lay down my life for the sheep' (John 10:11, 15). 'Greater love hath no man than this, that a man lay down his life for his friends . . . Ye are my friends . . .' (John 15:13).

The Cross is the symbol of our Lord's supreme giving of himself. The Incarnation itself, the Christ event from Christmas to the Crucifixion, is all giving of himself. To begin with he gives up his glory, his might, his majesty, his dominion and his power, all that glory which he had with the Father 'before the world was' (John 17:5). He lays it aside. He is 'despised and rejected by men' (Isa. 53:3). He totally divests himself and makes himself 'of no reputation':

Who, being in very nature God,
   did not consider equality with God something to be
      grasped,
but made himself nothing,
   taking the very nature of a servant,
   being made in human likeness.
And being found in appearance as a man,
   he humbled himself
   and became obedient to death – even death on a cross!
                              (Phil. 2:6–8 NIV)

Giving is loving in action, and in Jesus God gives himself totally. The Cross is the cost of loving, yet I am not happy with ideas of ransom and redemption which suggest that the cost which Christ paid was a price which was somehow demanded. With whom can God make a bargain? But the language of commerce is constantly used in the Bible: 'Ye are bought with a price' (1 Cor. 6:20); 'Forasmuch as ye know that ye were not redeemed with corruptible things, as silver and gold . . . but with the precious blood of Christ' (1 Peter 1:18, 19). We may say that some achievement costs someone great effort or costs him his life; that cost is not paid to anyone. So Christ's love for man cost him his life and death; and the fruit of his love is given as a free gift which we could not earn.

We have seen the Cross as God's culminating giving of himself. The Crucifixion is like a great document sealed in blood – the covenant, the testament, of our new relationship with God is sealed in the blood of the Cross. The Crucifixion is past and over, yet the crucifix is always there before our eyes. It is the perpetual assurance that nothing can separate us from the love of God. Some theologians have said that persistent sin can separate us from the love of God; but this is what St Paul wrote to the Romans:

Who shall separate us from the love of Christ? Shall distress, or persecution, or famine, or nakedness, or peril, or the sword? . . . Nay, in all these things we are more than conquerors through him that loved us. For I am persuaded that neither death, nor life, nor angels, nor principalities, nor powers, nor things present, nor things to come, nor height, nor depth, nor any other creature, shall be able to separate us from the love of God which is in Christ Jesus our Lord. (Rom. 8:35–9)

Isn't that gorgeous!

Drawing All Men

Let us return to the image of the brazen serpent. In John 13:14 Jesus says: 'As Moses lifted up the serpent in the wilderness, even so must the Son of man be lifted up.' Then later, in John 12:32, he refers back to this, saying: 'I, if I be lifted up from the earth, will draw all men unto me.' Consider the drawing power of the Cross.

All through the Bible we see God reaching out to draw us to himself and the Cross is the final act, the final throw as it were, in God's bid for man. He had been bidding for man down the centuries and this is the climax of his action. We have looked at the beginning of man's sin – Adam's sin – and at God's response; and here in the Crucifixion is the final demonstration, the climax of God's searching and yearning.

We hear God's longing in the Reproaches, a traditional service for Holy Week: 'O my people, what have I done unto thee, or wherein have I wearied thee? Answer me. Answer me' (Mic. 6:3). You may know the form in the Anglican prayers for Good Friday where the refrain runs: 'My people, what wrong have I done to you? What good have I not done to you? Listen to me.' (LHWE, p. 208).

God is still longing for us. Why don't we respond? In Matthew's account of the beginning of Holy Week, Jesus himself says: 'O Jerusalem, Jerusalem, you who kill the prophets and stone those sent to you . . . how often would I have gathered your children together, as a hen gathers her chicks under her wings, but you would not' (Matt. 23:37).

Consider for a moment the great and deep tenderness of God. There are many tender mother-like aspects of God; we cannot deny the suggestion of the hen with her chickens. The Psalmist has the same picture: 'He shall defend thee under his wings, and thou shalt be safe under his feathers' (Ps. 91:4). Our prayerbook consecration prayer begins: 'Almighty God our heavenly Father, who of thy tender mercy didst give thine only Son Jesus Christ to suffer death upon the Cross for our redemption . . .' This is not mercy towards Jesus, who had to suffer; the tender mercy is towards us in allowing Jesus to suffer for us. We need to recognize God's tender mercy and, in consequence, the need to show mercy ourselves.

Isaiah brings out this tenderness:

> Can a mother forget the baby at her breast
> and have no compassion on the baby she has borne?
> Though she may forget, I will not forget you!
> See, I have engraved you on the palms of my hands.
>
> (Isa. 49:15)

Our names are graven on the palms of his hands – and here is a double meaning. We know that the wounds in his hands served to authenticate the risen body of Christ. He showed them to his disciples. He told Thomas to touch the wounds in his hands and his side, the proofs of his Resurrection and his love for us. Charles Wesley pictured our Lord interceding for us:

> Before the throne my Saviour stands,
> My Friend and Advocate appears;
> My name is graven on his hands,
> And him the Father always hears.   (MHB 232)

I have an idea which you may find rather far-fetched. If you don't find it helpful you needn't take any notice of it. I have thought of God's relation with man as a kind of card game in which God makes his final bid for man. It has been said that Jesus is the King of Hearts, and Hearts are trumps of course, and the trump card is the Ace of Hearts which is the Cross. It is the final card which God puts down. Nothing can defeat the crucified Christ.

Entering the Jigsaw

What was Christ doing there on the Cross? My next point is difficult but I believe it is a valid insight which gives us a glimpse into the mystery of the Cross. Our redemption is like the treasure hid in the field. It is a pearl of great price, but we have to dig round and search for its meaning.

'The Crucifixion is God being hung up on the hook of his own creation.' This was said to me by a priest; I do not know whether it was his own or a quotation, but it sums up the view I am thinking about. God is hanging there in his incarnate manhood. The idea goes like this: God created all things and God saw everything that he had made and behold that it was very good (Gen. 1:31). He did not create evil. But evil is a fact of life; it came into existence though we can't really explain how or why. But in creating our freewill God obviously took a risk and limited his own freewill. So therefore God is responsible for the fact that evil exists. It exists with his permission and he finds the agony of this intolerable. We too find it intolerable when we see the innocent suffer, and know that children die in their millions. God who loves more than we love must find it even more intolerable than we find it. We are less responsible for things than God is; he must suffer the extra agony of knowing that he is responsible. But what can he do about it?

God limited his own infinite power by creating this finite universe. In creating as he did he, as it were, tied his own hands. There are things which are evil and terrible, but we may ask how God could have righted them. Should he have brought his world to an end? Scrapped the whole thing? Wiped out the past and started again? Would it have been an act of love to negate his creation? To forget those who had striven to do good and had loved him? To wipe out the past, which contained good as well as bad? Should he wipe out Abraham, Zoroaster, and Buddha? Should he wipe out the saints and Mother Teresa? And if God started over again, could he have created anything but a similar creation; similar, that is, in being a universe in which man was free to love him, and so one in which men were free to turn from him? I think he could only create a similar universe.

So God is stuck with his own creation which involves sin, suffering, and death. And the only thing he can do is to enter and go right deep down into his own creation, into the agony of sin and suffering and death, and deal with it from the inside. And it is because he is acting inside our limitations that we cannot see clearly just what he is doing on the Cross or how he is doing it.

This is no explanation of the mystery which we cannot explain. But it is a statement of my understanding of how sin and suffering and death come within the providence of God and are not facts outside his purpose and his love. 'God made him who had no sin to be sin for us, so that in him we might become the righteousness of God' (2 Cor. 5:21 NIV) The fullest depth of evil is embraced by Jesus on the Cross. And by God how it hurts!

You can look at life itself as a great jigsaw puzzle. (Though there is a difference between a mystery and a puzzle.) You may think of the mysteries of life and death and the purpose of things as bits to be fitted together in a way which gives them meaning. There are pieces which are hard to fit in – the agony here and the unknown cause of death there, or the child born deaf. A large piece of the puzzle seems to be missing. I am more and more convinced that the missing piece in the jigsaw, the awkward-shaped piece that you need to put in, is the Cross. Insert the Cross into the mysteries and there comes some sort of a pattern.

If I look up from my sin, from my own depths of panic, despair and darkness – if I look up from the world's agony, I keep seeing nothing but blinding blackness. But if I deliberately insert the Cross there, then somehow the pain, the suffering, the sin and the agony are there in the Cross. There's no kind of suffering that isn't there in the Cross. You look up and see nothing but blindness, but force the Cross into that picture and you see that things come together and they make a whole. I still don't see the clear meaning of it, but the Cross relates to every kind of evil, because in the Cross there is the suffering of God himself. Though I don't see the purpose of it all, I am able to discern that there is a purpose. If the Son of God is there then there is a purpose. I am confident that, when things seem meaningless, the Cross is the proof and demonstration that they have a meaning.

I started by seeing the Cross in the whole context of God's relationship with man from Genesis and the creation on. We see the whole great scheme in the prophets and the psalms and so on. Put the Cross there in its total context, then it comes into its own. Abraham and Moses, and all the prophets, the psalmists and the law – Christ is the context in which all things have happened. Christ is the key. And as we all know, Christ is risen. Alleluia!

5

Prayer with Christ Crucified

There are many crucifixions in our own day – that is to say, many people suffer rejection, injustice, torture and pain. For many the physical suffering is more prolonged than that of Jesus, but it is hard to think that anyone suffers worse mental torment than he did. The Christians who suffer are upheld by the sense that they are sharing an experience with our Lord and that Christ, who understands their plight, is praying for them. But many who suffer are without the sense of companionship at the Cross and it is the task of us who do have that sense of companionship to remember them there.

'When we survey the wondrous Cross', we may see it in the context of all eternity. But we are individuals who live our present lives here and now and have our own personal experience of the Cross. This is partly grounded in our reading and our prayer, in our imaginative understanding of the death of Jesus; but it is also grounded in our own lives and our knowledge of the lives of people of our own generation.

Many of these meditations grew out of Gonville's own religious life while it was centred in the Church of St Vedast. If one looks into the visitors' book there, one sees how often strangers have been struck by the prayerful atmosphere of the church. But this does not mean that the atmosphere of the church is totally other-worldly. There is a table which is always deep in current literature about today's problems, and about the societies and groups of people who work to alleviate them. These concerns are kept before us, for our action and for our prayers. There we may read about wars and the fear of wars, about the sick and the handicapped, about the starving and the underprivi-

leged. We are reminded of those who drink too much alcohol and those who have no pure water. Not least there is always something about the passion of Africa.

Gonville's days of imprisonment and interrogation, his months on remand and on trial, deepened his understanding of Christ's passion and gave him a new conviction of the love of God which lay behind it. Because his determination to preach 'Jesus Christ and him crucified' (1 Cor. 2:2) is related to his personal experience, we have included two talks which show him facing a particular crisis and preaching on a particular problem. The first is a talk about solitary confinement which was first given to a youth club; it was taped and later broadcast on the BBC World Service. The second is a sermon on apartheid which he preached in New York.

What Gonville has been through sharpens the edge of what he has to say about prayer. For most of us it is largely through our prayers that we are able to bring our understanding of the Cross to bear on our understanding of the present world. Here are some thoughts on the healing, supportive power of the Cross within today's tribulation and some simple counsel about the prayer of intercession.

Solitary Confinement

I have been and am concerned with the liberation of the black people of the Republic of South Africa. I do not believe that Jesus came just to save men's souls: I believe that he came to deliver man. I believe that the freedom of man is a necessary part of his development, and I know for a fact that under the apartheid system – which I regard as blasphemous against God and man – it is not possible for the African to rise to the dignity of manhood. And so I believe in fighting it with all the power at my command.

Because of what I did and said I was watched and was under some sort of strain for five or six years. And then finally the Security Police arrived in my flat and I was taken away into solitary confinement. Now solitary confinement cells are rather different from ordinary cells. In Rhodesia I ministered to men who were going to be hanged. I know what ordinary prison cells look like, but security cells are different. Around the steel door there is an inner steel grille, reaching from the ceiling to the floor, with another steel grille door, so that dangerous prisoners, like myself, can't attack the warder as he comes in, and your food can be handed through the grille to you.

Food isn't difficult to hand to you; it consists entirely of two pieces of dried bread in the morning for breakfast, two pieces of dried bread for lunch with a little bit of 'dog meat', and two pieces of dry bread for supper. And the only thing you have to drink is very, very sweetened coffee. No water. You can't get water unless you scream the place down for it. And we all believe – though I can't prove it – that the coffee is so sweet because it is drugged. You get hallucinations, and things begin to wave at you before you have been in there more than twenty-four hours. I had to have psychiatric treatment after my remand, and the psychiatrist seemed to agree that I couldn't have disintegrated as quickly as that unless there had been some sort of drug in the coffee.

So you go into this cell and it contains two things, a lavatory pan and a bed, and nothing else. There's nothing to sit on; there's no chair or table; you can sit on the concrete of course. You're not allowed to have anything to read. You don't take anything with you, no toothbrush. There is no water to wash in. You don't wash. You don't shave. You do nothing at all. You are just left there with absolutely nothing.

You know the psychology of the whole thing – you read about it in James Bond or if you read psychology; the idea is that you should become a nothing. Man needs above all things to relate. But you have no one to relate to. No warder will talk to you; you have no communication with anybody or anything. You have heard of prisoners making friends with birds and so on, because they are desperate to find something to relate to. They reduce you so that you are all unshaven and a mess and you begin to smell, and then they hope that you will cling, make a relationship with your interrogators: this is the point of this treatment.

So I was locked up in my cell. The lights are generally left on all night long. Sometimes this damned light is switched on and off all night. One particular night it wasn't switched on at all, as it was a night on which I had been asked a question. They sometimes do this, they ask you a question the answer to which means you're going to involve somebody – you've got to, there's no other answer to it – and they leave you with this all night, so you worry yourself sick about it. And you're given no light at all, so that – they know you are going to be awake anyway – you can find nothing even to look at, just the blank darkness of the cell. But all of this is what solitary confinement is, and there is no need to go into any more detail about it. You've read all about it. But what I want to point out is that this in fact does happen. It's not just stuff that you read about. It happens in South Africa. And I was a white man and was better treated than a black man.

I learned a good deal of things in that prison cell. The centre of my religion has always been the Mass, the Holy Communion, the service of the Eucharist – whatever you like to call it. And it is my belief – it need not necessarily be yours – that what I receive in the Holy Communion is not just bread and wine. I don't believe in magic. I believe it is bread, but it is not just bread; it is the living bread, the living bread which comes down from heaven, the physical means by which the living presence of the glorified Jesus is passed to me in physical, encapsulated form. I believe that what I receive is not just wine but the precious blood of Jesus: this is my belief about the Mass, and I've said Mass every morning of my life, while I've been a priest, except when I have been on holiday, and now when I have no church. But it has always been my custom; I've depended on it.

And so, on the very first morning – it wasn't difficult to get up early with the lights on all night – I got up. And in my cell there were two windows standing high up, and it was easy to stand there and imagine a great big cross, hanging down between them. And there I stood and I used to go through the words of the Holy Communion service in its South African form. If you have said it every day for thirty-five years, you remember it fairly well. And I would use the 23rd Psalm perhaps for an Epistle, and the beginning of St John's Gospel for the Gospel, or whatever, and say the prayers of the Mass, as best I could remember them.

And you know, it was a reality. 'Therefore with angels and archangels and all the whole company of heaven' – I don't think I have ever known the reality of the company of heaven as I did in that prison cell, I'd never even known what the Church was before, either. I used to have such a narrow view of the Church, as an Anglo-Catholic. Now I know the Church is the company of the beloved, whether they're Quakers, or Romans, or – what does it matter? I didn't know that the world was at prayer for me – I was in solitary confinement. I had no papers and nobody told me what was going on. But I was part of the company of the beloved of Christ.

I'm no mystic. I don't get any sense of the presence of God really. But I felt the presence of the Church, both in heaven and on earth. And then, when it came to the time of the consecration, I took – I didn't have any bread or wine – I took nothing in my hands and I said, 'This is my body, which is given for you. Do this in remembrance of me.' And again I took nothing in my hands and I said, 'This is the blood of the new testament which is shed for you and for many, for the remission of sins. Do this as often as ye shall drink it in remembrance of me.' And I'll tell you this, against all my whole teaching – as a bigoted Anglo-Catholic I suppose – it is my honest knowledge that the communions that I received there in that prison cell, without the means of bread and wine, were as real and as glorious and as triumphant and as magnificent as any communion I've ever received in my own cathedral, with the organ going and the incense and the bells and all the glory. Just as real and wholly as healing and as complete. That is my witness and my evidence.

Apartheid
(This is a sermon preached in New York in the mid-1970s. Sadly, it is not yet out of date.)

Our religion is concerned with one thing, with love. God is love and we thank him 'for all the blessings of this life'. That means love and laughter and spring, family and friends, and if you have been in prison like I have, above all things, the joy of just being free! Free to move about and know that you are not being watched by the security police all the time; being free to talk to people face to face without fear. Above all, our prayerbook says, we are grateful to God for his love in our redemption. 'God so loved the world that he gave his only begotten Son, so that all who believe in him should not perish but have everlasting life' (John 3:16).

'God so loved the world' – not God so loved the Church. God must get fed-up with the Church at times. I do anyway. It doesn't say God loved the English people, or the American people, or the black or the white people. God so loved the whole wide world and everyone in it that he gave himself for it. And we are all the object of God's love.

This redemption, this re-creation, is the gift of the Lord Jesus Christ. He came to be the redeemer. He came to make people whole. How often he said, 'Thy faith has made thee whole' – you poor dear, you've been in pieces, you've been broken by some disease; now faith has made you whole. Of course we are all broken. We are divided within ourselves, as St Paul said, 'The good that I would, I do not. The evil that I would not, that I do!' (Rom. 7:19). We are schizoid characters, unhealed. And God knows, we have broken man from man in so many ways. There are placed for house-owners here and for tenants there, for white here and black there. Wherever there are divisions, there we are diseased.

We are divided by sins. Some of these things are our own fault. Some of them we inherited through the sins of our forebears who left tragic situations that we can't alter. There are great powers that we don't seem able to manoeuvre or shift. We are caught up into a sinful state of things. We are not what we are meant to be. That is to say, free men, growing up into the measure of the stature of the fullness of Christ.

There is only one man who has ever been what man was meant to be – that is Jesus. Jesus is the man. He is, alone, the prototype of a human being. He is what we were meant to be. We are diminished and less than we are meant to be. He came to heal us and set us free not just from the results of sin but within our circumstances. Remember that when Jesus rose from the dead the marks of the power of sin were still in his wounded body. Bunyan, in prison, was set free, not from Bedford jail, but within Bedford jail. Whatever our circumstances Christ comes to set us free, to heal us through his love, and the love that he commands us to have for each other.

Jesus says: 'Thou shalt love.' You cannot be a full human being unless you love – and that's what you must get up with each morning – love, love, love. Whatever the cost may be thou shalt love. 'By this shall all men know that you are my disciples, that ye love one another' (John 13:35). This is how Christ's healing works – through our loving others and ministering their healing.

Among the most diminished of all the people who live on the face of the earth, among the most unloved, are the black people who live in an atmosphere of hatred in the so-called Republic of South Africa. They are the most diminished of all men, not allowed to act or to live as men, without vote or choice of what they want to be or want to do. They cannot live where they like or love where they like. One of our sub-deacons was put in jail for one month for being found in bed with his own wife – he had not got his permit to sleep in a house in a different part of Johannesburg. These people are not free but kept in a subjugated position while the white man keeps control.

The violence that is offered to the dignity of every black man whatever his state – the chief, the scholar, the servant, the slave – is a living blasphemy. I called the government blasphemers and acted against them as practically as I could. I gave money which I had borrowed from my friends to feed and clothe the wives and families of political prisoners – men who have tried to set their country free. As a result of that I was detained in solitary confinement in the Security Police cell at Vorster Square. I was interrogated by the Security Police. I was tried in the supreme court of justice of the Transvaal and I was found guilty of doing these things and I was sentenced to five years in prison. When I went on appeal to the supreme court of South Africa I was declared in fact to be innocent. I believe that because of all this I have a right to talk about South Africa – about its needs, its desperate condition and, too, about love.

We Christians have the only true picture of love. Love has never been demonstrated fully and wholly except through Christians who see it up there on the Cross. That is the only kind of love – something that bleeds and and dies and is wholly given to the object of love. That is the only kind of love which can overcome, and it is a violent and bloody kind of love. But this is what we are called to.

One of the great Christian words which echoes the word 'love' is the Greek word *koinonia*. It is a magnificent strong word, but the usual translation, 'fellowship', sounds like a bun and a cup of tea after church. *Koinonia* means something much deeper than this, a belonging together and a need of each other; I am wholly a part of you; we are bound together in the body of Christ and by our beginning to grow together in love for each other. This is community, *koinonia*, the coming togetherness.

The Church calls us to love one another: 'Beloved, let us love one another' (1 John 4:7). Let us grow together. Over against the Christian church we have the Southern African government which says: 'No! No! Not together – APART! Apartheid! Apartness! Be separate!' The word apartheid is the exact opposite of the Christian gospel. And it doesn't just separate black from white, it means separating a black man from his brother black man, separating the tribes, the Zulu from the Xhosa and the Xhosa from the Venda. It means separating the men from the women; keeping the women out in the country and bringing the men into the towns to work as migrant labourers. Separate! Divide! Divide and rule! Divide the families, divide the people! This is the destruction of any kind of coming togetherness. So you have a church which preaches *koinonia* and a state which says: Apart!

What has this to do with us? We are brothers and sisters in blood, all of us. Black or white, we are brothers in Christ. We should be concerned about our whole relationship to the country of South Africa, in commerce, in sport, in friendship. We should use any influence or clout that we have on behalf of the African.

I believe that the whole apartheid concept, which has been supported by the Dutch Reformed Church, has a theological background; the black man has been seen as a lesser creation. I believe this is utterly evil, that it has in it elements of the demonic, the satanic. 'We wrestle not against flesh and blood – it is against principalities, against powers, against the rulers of the darkness of this world, against spiritual wickedness in high places' (Eph. 6:12). Jesus himself said, 'This kind cometh not out except by prayer and fasting' (Matt. 17:21). So I call you to prayer and fasting for Africa. Be concerned and informed so that you know their hurts and can pray with your head and your heart. It is only love that is going to cure this thing and make South Africa whole.

Praying with Both Hands

I am very firmly convinced of the power of prayer – not least of intercession. I have experienced this in, and on, my own life – not least when I was in trouble in South Africa. I have written about how, in solitary confinement in the Security Police Head-quarters in John Vorster Square in Johannesburg, I was aware, not so much of the presence of God, as of the presence and power of the intercessions being made for me. It was only after my release that I read and heard in the news of the very wide interest and concern for me, and this tied in with the experience I had felt in prison. But I have had, as I expect all Christians have, other experiences of the effectiveness of intercession in times of trouble, sickness, and so on, not only in my own life but on the lives of others.

My own view of how intercession may work is, I expect, a little jejeune; but it seems to be satisfactory for me, though I suspect that the truth is much more wonderful! I know that God *is*, and that he is the omnipotent and loving creator of all life and of all things. It seems to me that, in creating the creation, he limits himself to and by the finite nature of the beings and things that he creates. He further limits himself by giving a measure of freewill to his created beings. So he is, as it were, in his heaven, longing for peace and power and plenty to be poured out onto the creation. But he is prevented from that outpouring by the creation – especially by the selfish wills of men. Intercession, it seems to me, is when we align ourselves with the will of God, longing as he does for his peace and healing to pour into the world, and so enabling, allowing that to happen.

It seems to me that intercession is a form or mode of incarnation. Our Lord identified himself wholly and completely with man, right down to the basic things which he shared with man in his passion, in his death, and even in his passing deep down into the place of the departed. The more we identify ourselves, as deeply and fully as we possibly can, with those for whom we intercede, living and departed, the more real our intercession will be.

When we seek to make ourselves channels through which our Lord's love and power may flow, we must seek, on the one hand, to identify with and connect as directly as possible with those for whom we are praying; and, on the other hand, to identify with God, with Christ, to whom we intercede. We have one hand in theirs and one hand in his. Both hands need to hold firm and fast. The personal holiness of the intercessor, his personal grip of the hand of God, must count for a good deal towards the power and effectiveness of the prayer.

In our prayers we have our personal responsibilities or vocations. I think of identifying myself with my particular constituency – that is the group or the area with which I am identified. There are broad constituencies and categories: I am human, I am a sinner, I am saved, I am a Christian, I am a priest, I am retired. And there are closer ones: I belong to the Servants of Christ the King, to Tower Hamlets, to my family of friends, to this household where I live. I identify also with the sick and the suffering, the lonely, the fearful, the unwanted, the inadequate, the failures. My constituencies are my concerns.

I once saw a building in West Virginia which was known locally as the 'Martinsburg Monster'. This housed a great computer which stored the personal details of every citizen of the United States. A computer made by man – one of the things man makes because of his God-given intelligence – may serve as a model for something about our relationship with God in our prayer. The machine can single out a single fact from many millions with speed and particular accuracy. It may suggest that we do not have to spend a long time in thinking of each individual and his situation. We may name him or her, we just touch the button as it were, and that releases God's power.

One often begins an act of prayer, 'In the name of the Father and the Son and the Holy Spirit'. We may offer this prayer on behalf of one of our constituencies, adding, 'and in the name of Africa' – or of whoever we want to pray for.

Our Father

I am sometimes asked if I can say something simple and practical about praying for other people, especially about praying for Africa. Intercession need not be a special way of praying. Any of our prayers can simply be offered on behalf of someone whom we have in mind, without there being any need to enlarge on the problems of the situation. Sometimes we want to say something more special, or to express our concern by holding it up for a little longer.

The Lord's prayer can give us a simple way into intercession. 'Our Father, which art in heaven' – and I tend to add 'and in Tredegar Square'. As you may add 'in Lechlade' or 'in New York', or wherever you happen to be, physically or in imagination. God's presence about those for whom we pray forms a background to our prayer: he is there and as ready to act in Johannesburg or Calcutta as in London or Canterbury.

So in the 'Thy' (or 'Your') petitions which follow, we can make the request more specific by adding a name. 'Hallowed be thy name' – in Africa. 'Thy Kingdom come' – in Africa.

'Thy will be done' – in Africa. The next part is about 'us' but again we may be more specific, asking not merely, 'Give us this day our daily bread,' but give the starving in Africa or India their daily bread.

'Forgive us our trespasses as we forgive those who trespass against us.' May Black and White find mutual forgiveness. Forgive us our trespasses onto forbidden territory. 'Lead us not into temptation' – preserve South Africa from the temptations to hatred and revenge.

I think it is worthwhile to make a real emphasis on 'us', remembering the great need which we have of each other and the given-ness of belonging together. We belong to each other in the first instance through our creation, as fellow human beings. More especially, as Christians, we belong to each other through our redemption; we are in Christ together with each other, inextricably linked.

I believe that all prayer is intercessory, that is, it has an intercessory value. Every act of adoration that I may make, every lifting up of the heart or hands in prayer, must lift up the creation and God's creatures, especially my brothers and sisters in Christ with whom I am linked. The word 'communion' means that we and Christ are brought together in that sacrament. 'Abide in me and I in you' (John 15:4) – a relationship which parallels Christ's own relationship with the Father, 'I and the Father are one' (John 10:30). The Eucharist is the greatest form of intercession because it connects with our Lord and his prayer in heaven where 'he ever liveth to make intercession for them' (Heb. 7:25).

Many prayers are addressed to the Father and end, 'through Jesus Christ his Son our Lord'; thus, rightly, they stress that Jesus stands as mediator, 'facing both ways', as he identifies himself with the Father, as his Son, and with us as fellow human beings. As he prays for us to the Father, we too face both ways, towards our fellows for whom we intercede and towards him in whose care and prayer we place them.

If even these suggestions seem complicated, remember that 'Lord, have mercy' says all that needs to be said. But it needs to be repeated and meant.

Now and to the End of the Ages

Our last chapter looks past the Cross to Easter and Ascension. The first piece reflects the traditional services for Easter night. The texts are accessible in Roman Catholic forms or in the Anglican book of services and prayers, Lent, Holy Week, Easter. *The ancient rite includes readings from Scripture about the mighty acts of God, beginning with the story of the creation. The Service of Light (at late night or early morning) proclaims the Resurrection in spoken word and dramatic ceremony. A light is lit outside the darkened church and the Easter candle is lit at the entrance and brought in, in procession, with the pronouncement, 'The light of Christ!' The people light candles from the Easter candle and all the lights in the church are lit. The Easter Liturgy often includes a baptism and renewal of baptismal vows; then follows the first Easter Eucharist.*

Easter is a bridge between Good Friday and Ascension Day. We end trying to stretch our minds to grasp how Christ's work in time leads up to his work in eternity.

Light and Life

I love the Easter services. I enjoy reading the first chapter of Genesis, 'In the beginning God' – in the beginning there was God, only God and nothing but God! And 'God created the heaven and earth' – possibly in some sort of 'big bang'. Before it 'the earth was without form and void'. There was empty chaos and 'darkness was upon the face of the deep'. We are reminded of the emptiness of Good Friday, when the disciples had forsaken their master and fled, and 'there was darkness over all the earth until the ninth hour' (Matt. 27:45). Then Genesis continues: 'The Spirit of God moved upon the face of the waters.' Chaos became cosmos. As science tells us, life emerged from the waters.

The readings at the Easter Vigil show us other moments when new life arose from the water: as in the story of Noah when he and his cargo of living creatures emerged from the ark to restock the earth (Gen. 8:17). As at the Red Sea when the Lord's strong wind drove back the water, that Moses and the escaping Israelites might go on dry ground through the sea, towards their new life in the promised land (Exod. 14:21–2). As in the prophecy of Ezekiel where God promises the Israelites, captive in Babylon, 'I will sprinkle clean water over you, and you shall be cleansed from all that defiles you . . . I will give you a new heart and put a new spirit within you' (Ezek. 36:25, 26).

So this night, at Easter midnight, the Spirit of God moved over the tomb; and the new life, the risen life, the resurrection body of Christ burst blazing out of the solid rock. As in Genesis God said, 'Let there be light, and there was light', so tonight we have lit the light of Christ. The paschal candle is burning and all have lit their candles from the light of Christ. His light has come to each of us as the light of the Easter gospel has shone through the world.

We think too of the water from which life first emerged. Not only is water the source and spring of life but its streams sustain life. I think of the green strip through brown desert where the Nile feeds the land of Egypt. I think of Ezekiel's picture of the river which will flow from the Temple, 'and everything shall live whither the river cometh' (Ezek. 47:9). He pictures the river of life, as we bless the font as the fountain of life.

We thank you that through the deep waters
   of death you brought your Son, and raised him to life in
      triumph.
Bless this water that your servants

who are washed in it may be made one with Christ in his
death and his resurrection . . .   (ASB, p. 231)

It is fitting at this time to look back to our own baptism:

As we celebrate the resurrection of our Lord Jesus Christ
from the dead, we remember that through the paschal
mystery we have died and been buried with him in baptism,
so that we may rise with him to a new life within the family
of his Church.   (LHWE, p. 234)

Our baptism is the source of our new life, our resurrection life,
our life in Christ which sustains our eternal life. And at your
Easter Eucharist you receive the glorious Body and the
precious Blood to 'preserve thy body and soul unto everlasting
life' (BCP).

Encounters

I expect it is right and proper for the Church to rejoice at
Easter with bells and song and triumphant music. But at the
first Easter night the grave was silent. In the darkness of the
night the soldier guards may have been aware of something
that made them fear. They fled as the wounded body, dead, and
pierced by the soldier's spear, was transformed, transfigured,
transmuted into the transcendent beauty of the risen resurrection body of Christ. There was no one to record how it
happened. Who could report the living Son of God bursting,
blasting from the solid rock in blinding, blazing glory – the
glory which he had with the Father 'before the world was'?
(John 17.5). And in the morning there was just the pile of
graveclothes lying there and the tomb full of just emptiness.

What we do have is a number of accounts of people's experi-
ences afterwards, of their encounters with the living Christ.
The first summary of these was written by St Paul before the
Gospels were written.

For what I received I passed on to you as of first importance:
that Christ died for our sins according to the Scriptures, that

he was buried, that he was raised on the third day according to the Scriptures, and that he appeared to Peter, and then to the Twelve. After that, he appeared to more than five hundred of the brothers at the same time, most of whom are still living, though some have fallen asleep. Then he appeared to James, then to all the apostles, and last of all he appeared to me also, as to one abnormally born.   (1 Cor. 15:3–8 NIV)

The Gospels contain three accounts of Christ's encounters with individuals: his meeting with Mary Magdalene when she came early to the tomb (John 20:11–18); his meeting with the disciples on the road to Emmaus (Luke 24:13–35); and his meeting with Thomas in the upper room (John 20:24–9).

Christ's first meeting was not with the 'Church' but with Mary in the garden. A woman's word was not accepted as legal witness in a Jewish court, but Mary's witness has come to us down the years. 'Jesus saith unto her, "Mary". She turned herself, and saith unto him, "Rabboni"; which is to say, "Master".'

There were the disciples who were walking to Emmaus and discussing their doubts. They were joined, it seemed, by a stranger. But at supper they knew him 'in the breaking of bread', as we may know him in the Eucharist.

Then there was Thomas who could not believe what the other disciples told him, not until he had seen and touched his Lord for himself. But when Jesus greeted him in the upper room he knew that it was Jesus. And perhaps he understood more deeply than them all when he said, 'My Lord, my God!'

At the end of Paul's account of the resurrection experiences there is his curious little addendum, 'and last of all was seen of me also as of one born out of due time' (AV). He claimed that he too saw Jesus and heard him, at midday, in blinding, blazing light. And that encounter turned Saul the Pharisee into Paul the Apostle.

The Easter message is not normally proclaimed crashingly and compellingly, to compel belief by a blaze of blinding glory, but gently and gradually, one to one, person to person. I

suppose it is generally through some sort of experience, probably not so dramatic as St Paul's, that we ourselves encounter
Christ, and some still small voice tells us that he is risen. Jesus
comes to us in quiet communion. He meets us as individuals,
as John or Mary. And we answer, 'My Lord, my God.'

King and Priest

Our own mental icons of Holy Week are largely based on our
reading of the Bible and on the Church's rich tradition of
liturgical worship. I think of the places where I have served,
mostly in town churches and cathedrals. At St Vedast's the
Holy Week ceremonial was full and traditional. Friends often
camped in the vicarage so that they could see the whole
sequence through from the evening of Maundy Thursday to
the Easter Eucharist.

Vera's memories are mostly more rural. Last year she joined
a Palm Sunday procession, not round a church with banners
and incense, but up a sunny Oxfordshire churchyard golden
with wild daffodils. Another year she watched a 'crucifixion'
acted out through stormy rain in an East Coast market place.
She remembers especially a Good Friday address at Whit-
church-on-Thames. The Rector described the events in Jerusalem with the vividness of a journalist just back from the first
century. He then spoke of the majesty of the Crucifixion –
how from that moment we see Christ's power stretching out
everywhere and for all time. He quoted Venantius Fortunatus'
great hymn in which he calls the Cross the 'Tree of Glory':

> Fulfilled is now what David told
> In true prophetic song of old,
> How God the heathen's King should be:
> For God is reigning from the Tree.
> (*Vexilla Regis prodeunt*, AMR 96)

Jesus is sometimes shown on a crucifix 'reigning from the
Tree'. The hymn was known in this country before the Norman
conquest and it is illustrated in the Saxon crucifix against the

porch at Langford, a village church in Oxfordshire. Here Christ stands against the Cross wearing a simple cassock. His head was broken off in an age of desecration but tradition knows that it was crowned. Here is Christ as Redeemer, Priest and King. It is a timeless image of Jesus Christ 'the same yesterday, today and for ever' (Heb. 13:8).

At Ascension time we stress our Lord's kingship. In his earthly life his supporters had once tried to seize him and make him king, but he had evaded them (John 6:15). The only time when he was called 'King' was by the mocking soldiers who, with macabre ferocity, 'stripped him and put a scarlet robe on him, and then twisted together a crown of thorns and set it on his head'. They spat in his face and hailed him 'King of the Jews' (Matt. 27:28–30). But on Ascension Day we think of him as King indeed – 'King of kings and Lord of lords'.

> The head that once was crowned with thorns
>   Is crowned with glory now;
> A royal diadem adorns
>   The mighty Victor's brow.
>
> The highest place that heaven affords
>   Is his, is his by right,
> The King of Kings, and Lord of Lords,
>   And heaven's eternal Light.
>   (T. Kelly, AMR 218)

In my study there is another crucifix which brings out the same timeless and eternal significance of the Crucifixion. Again Jesus stands against the Cross. He is not hanging in torment; he is in command and holds out his arms as in an inclusive welcome: 'He opened wide his arms for us on the cross . . .' (Hippolytus, 3rd century, ASB p. 40).

The vestments he wears are more obviously priestly than the cassock-like garment of the Saxon Christ. This is the high priestly Christ of the Epistle to the Hebrews 'who sat down at the right hand of the throne of the Majesty in heaven; and who serves in the sanctuary, the true tabernacle set up by the Lord, not by man' (Heb. 8:1–2). This is the High Priest of the new covenant who offers no sacrifice of the blood of goats and bulls but who 'offered himself unblemished to God (Heb. 9:14) . . . once for all at the end of the ages to do away with sin by the sacrifice of himself' (Heb. 9:26). This is Jesus 'made like his brothers in every way, in order that he might become a merciful and faithful high priest' who 'because he himself suffered when he was tempted, he is able to help those who are being tempted' (Heb. 2:17–18). This is Christ who 'is able to save completely those who come to God through him, because he always lives to intercede for them' (Heb. 7:25). And this is the Jesus who still says to us in the Communion, 'This cup is the new covenant in my blood . . . whenever you eat this bread and drink this cup you proclaim the Lord's death until he comes' (1 Cor. 11:26).

Lift Your Eyes

On Ascension Day we should lift up our eyes and lift up our hearts to see Jesus the Saviour in triumph and glory. That will help us to get things into proportion. If we look at the world and ourselves, we are bound to get depressed. We make such a mess of things. Looking up to heaven is not escapism, for heaven actually is the reality. That is where we belong. That is where we have meaning. That is the point of the Ascension. The Ascension is for us. Jesus said, 'I go to prepare a place for you' (John 14:3). That will be your place, not anyone's place. 'It is for you that I go away and I will send you another Comforter' (John 14:16). Our Lord the Spirit will be with us in our journey through the world, and afterwards we will be with Christ. That is the message of Ascension Day. It helps us to see things in the right proportion and in perspective.

'God so loved the world, that he gave his only begotten Son, that whosoever believeth in him should not perish, but have everlasting life' (John 3:16). 'The word was made flesh' (John 1:14) and dwelt among us to live for us and die for us. The climax came on the Cross; that is the breakthrough. Life meets death; good meets evil; and love meets hate. At the crashing cry, '*Tetelestai*!' ('It is finished!'), the climax is sealed. In a blinding creative flash within the tomb the body of Christ was transfigured, transmuted, metamorphosed into new life, into a new dimension, a new continuum. We don't know how it happened, but in the tomb that transformation took place into the resurrection body, which is the ascension body.

But of course there is still more to be done. Jesus has to complete the circle, the link. He brought his godhead to earth that he might take our manhood into heaven, completing the breakthrough.

> Mighty Lord, in thine Ascension
> We by faith behold our own.   (AMR 148)

We celebrate Ascension Day remembering his birth for us, his death for us, his Resurrection for us, and his Ascension for us. 'It is expedient for you that I go away' (John 16:7). He drives home that he is not leaving his disciples behind without the promise of his Spirit who will be in them to guide and encourage them. 'Where two or three are gathered together in my name, there am I in the midst of them' (Matt. 18:20). 'I am with you always even unto the end of the world' (Matt. 28:20). His promise of his presence means that the Ascension is not an end except in so far as it is a beginning. He leaves one mode or part of his work and begins the final dispensation. He cannot change his love or his saving work but he sets them free. He enables his love to flow more freely. The paradox is that by appearing to go into heaven, he becomes more present with all men everywhere. He is 'closer than hands and feet', and 'the traffic of Jacob's ladder is pitched between heaven and Charing Cross'. By going to heaven he is not cut off from time and space; instead he is able to join us here at any time.

(We need not get confused with the geography of heaven and the Ascension. Of course there isn't any geography. He had to show that this dispensation had ended. He disappears on the mountain but heaven is not a place somewhere away; it is a state of being with God. Being in love is a very real state but it has no geography; it is nothing to do with being in any physical place. Similarly we need not bother where heaven is;

heaven is all about us; heaven permeates the universe and the galaxies. Where Love is there is heaven.)

Lift up your eyes unto the hills. He that is and was and is to come promises, 'Surely I come quickly' (Rev. 22:20).

Alpha and Omega

On Ascension Day we think of Christ's return to his Father. What this means is beyond our knowledge but of course we may wonder about it. John's vision, the book of Revelation, is a great poem of wonder which may help us to sense the glory of that return. I advise you to read Revelation at this time. It is quite a short book and there are some glorious bits in it, like the angels round about the throne of God who numbered 'ten thousand times ten thousand, and thousands of thousands' (Rev. 5:11).

There are some rather tricky bits too, about Gog and Magog and the number 666. It's rather like a stew with some gristly bits in it. Don't choke on them; put them aside and go on reading the glorious bits.

I want to show you some of the pictures and visions of our Lord himself as John sees him. He is Alpha and Omega, the first and the last, the beginning and the end. Within that overall picture there are lots of lesser visions. I will remind you of some of them. 'I, John,' he wrote,

> saw seven golden candlesticks; and I saw in the midst of the seven candlesticks one like unto the Son of man, clothed with a garment down to his feet, girt about with a golden girdle; his head and his hair were white like wool, as white as snow; his eyes were as a flame or fire; and his feet were like fine brass as if they burnt in a furnace; and his voice as the sound of many waters. He had in his right hand seven stars, and out of his mouth went a sharp two-edged sword, and his countenance was as the sun shining in its strength.   (Rev. 1:12–16)

Another picture is of the throne which is set in heaven.

One sat on the throne and he was, to look upon, like a jasper and a sardine stone. And there was a rainbow round about the throne which looked like an emerald . . . And out of the throne proceeded lightnings and thunderings and voices . . . And before the throne there was a sea of glass like unto crystal.   (Rev. 4:2–6)

He goes on to see Christ as an extraordinary paradox: the lion and the lamb. He is the lion of the tribe of Judah – very very tough, raging and ramping round the world. He is also the lamb of God and very tender indeed.

And here is another vision:

I saw heaven opened and behold a white horse; and he that sat upon the horse was called Faithful and True . . . His eyes were as a flame of fire and on his head were many crowns and he had a name written, that no man knew, but he himself. And he was clothed with a vesture dipped in blood. And his name is called the Word of God . . . And out of his mouth goes a sharp sword . . . and he treads the winepress of the wrath of Almighty God. And he has a name written on his vesture and on his thigh: KING OF KINGS, AND LORD OF LORDS.   (Rev. 19:11–16)

The overall impression, from the first chapter to the last chapter, is of the timelessness and the totality of Christ. He is the first begotten of the dead, begotten of his Father before all worlds. His being encloses all time; he is and was and is to come. 'As it was in the beginning, is now, and shall be for ever' runs through the book like a refrain. The glory of our Lord was the same in the beginning as it is now in heaven where Christ reigns and ever shall be. 'The glory that I had with thee before the world was' (John 17:5). He is 'the same yesterday, today, and for ever' (Heb. 13:8). The glorious Christ spans all history from the beginning, the creation, to the end which is still to come. He includes it all, all time, all eternity. We are reminded of Julian of Norwich who saw in a vision that everything that God has created, which of course includes time, is just a tiny thing like a hazel nut in his hand.

AMEN.